ORIENTAL DISHES

by

JO LOGAN

Illustrated by Ian Jones

A THORSONS WHOLEFOOD COOKBOOK

THORSONS PUBLISHERS LIMITED
Wellingborough, Northamptonshire

First published 1984

British Library Cataloguing in Publication Data

Logan, Jo
   Oriental dishes.
   1. Cookery, Oriental
   I. Title
   641.595 TX724.5.A1

ISBN 0-7225-0787-9

Printed in Great Britain by
Richard Clay (The Chaucer Press) Ltd,
Bungay, Suffolk

ORIENTAL DISHES

Combines the exciting flavours and techniques of the East with healthy
wholefood ingredients to make dishes that are nutritious, delicious
— and a little bit different!

CONTENTS

INTRODUCTION

The staple diet in the Far East is rice, noodles and pulses, supplemented with local vegetables, nuts and fruit, fish and meat. Most of the recipes in this book were collected in Malaysia which, being a multi-racial society, offers a wide choice of Chinese, Malay, Indonesian and Indian cuisine. Such a society is, of course, also a multi-religious one, each with its own strict culinary taboos, and a high percentage of the population is vegetarian. Also, dairy herds are practically non-existent in the East, so the majority of these recipes are suitable for vegans as well as vegetarians.

The major difficulty in the compilation of any Oriental cookery book, however, is quoting exact quantities. Weights and measures are seldom used by Oriental cooks who are inclined to use a handful of this, a thumb twist of that, according to personal whim. The proportions of the various ingredients in a recipe tend, therefore, to depend almost entirely on the taste and judgement of the cook.

So, do experiment: you will soon learn to recognize the nature of the various ingredients and will then be able to adjust the quantities to suit your taste. After all, what I consider to be a perfectly balanced Sweet and Sour Sauce may not be exactly to your taste; you may prefer it a little saltier, more vinegary or whatever. That is really the fun of Oriental cooking: investing a particular dish with one's individuality by making amendments to the recipe so that what is produced is your Nasi Goreng — and not mine.

One word of advice, though, if you are unfamiliar with Oriental cookery it is not a good idea to try out a new dish when entertaining important guests. It can be very embarrassing to find oneself in the position of wondering whether or not the dish being prepared is supposed to be that rather peculiar shade of green when the boss and his wife are already seated at table!

If you are planning to give a dinner party and wish to do so in the Oriental manner, there are one or two points to bear in mind. The first is that the whole attitude towards eating is different in the Far East, where it is usual to sample small quantities of several different dishes rather than to glut oneself on only one or two as we tend to do in the West. Even the simplest Chinese family meals, for instance, will consist of five or six dishes (three or four entrées, rice and/or noodles, followed by a soup); a more formal dinner will comprise at least a dozen courses; while a banquet may run to thirty or forty dishes.

The emphasis is different, too. Basically, Oriental meals consist of very simple ingredients which are carefully selected and prepared so that their natural texture, colour and flavour are retained. Also, of course, cutlery is regarded as belonging strictly in the kitchen, not on the dining table, so most food is cut into bite-sized morsels before it is cooked.

This all means that Oriental cookery requires a maximum of preparation and a minimum of cooking time. There is one great advantage in this fact: it enables even an inexperienced cook to serve meals in the traditional Eastern manner — with far more dishes than in the West — by exercising a little common sense and considering the menu carefully before preparations are made.

All the recipes in this book are suitable for Eastern or Western eating methods.

If dining in the Oriental way, a dinner for four people would need four cold or side dishes (usually placed on the table before the guests are seated); four main dishes; at least one soup course; and rice or noodles accompanied by dipping sauces. Desserts, if included, are usually inserted at the beginning or middle of a meal, never at the end, although a dessert soup may be served. More usually, though, tea (without milk, sugar or lemon) will be served after a meal. Allow two extra dishes for each additional guest.

If eating Western style, two people should find one soup, two main dishes and a dessert adequate for an average meal. The order and number of dishes is, of course, up to you and plates, spoons and forks can be substituted if you feel unable to cope with rice bowls and chopsticks (although these aren't nearly as difficult to use as one might imagine).

But, whatever method of dining is preferred, a word or two about kitchen utensils and cooking methods may prove helpful. One item that will be found in any Oriental kitchen is a wok (*krahai* or *kwali*), a round-bottomed, deep pan with a lid, used for frying, sautéeing and boiling.

The best woks are made of cast-iron and, like omelette pans, should never be washed in soapy water but merely wiped out after use. Wok stands — metal rings similar to those used by caterers to separate stacked plates of cooked food — are easily obtainable, so these invaluable cooking utensils can be used on gas or electric cookers.

Always heat the wok before adding the oil whenever ingredients are to be fried, braised, sautéed or browned. Peanut oil is the most commonly used oil for cooking purposes and this is relatively inexpensive; sesame oil can also be used, although it does impart a slightly nutty flavour to the food, and this has been specified in some recipes. The oil should be heated until it is thin and easy-flowing before the ingredients to be cooked are added.

Should the addition of oil or water be required during the cooking process, pour this down the side of the wok and, unless stated otherwise in the recipe, heat water before it is added. When adding a sauce or gravy, make a well in the centre of the ingredients, exposing the bottom of the wok, and pour the sauce into this hollow. Once the sauce is slightly warm, it can be stirred in to the other ingredients.

Very little liquid is used in the majority of Oriental dishes since the traditional quick cook method brings out the natural flavour of vegetables without spoiling their colour or texture. In the East, the appearance and aroma of food are considered as important as flavour and even simple family meals are attractively presented.

Unless cooked foods are delicate enough to be broken into small pieces with chopsticks, ingredients are cut or chopped before being cooked. Oriental cooks believe in letting the weight of their cutting implements do the work, so use larger, much heavier knives than we do in the West. A rolling action is used when cutting vegetables such as carrots or cucumbers: a heavy knife or cleaver held at an angle is used to chop the vegetable which is then rolled before the second cut is made, rolled again before the third cut, and so on. Interesting shapes result and this method has the added advantage of preventing the vegetable slices from sticking together when cooked as they tend to do when all cut at the same angle.

Old-fashioned steamers — the kind where the bottom of the top pan is perforated, or the open rack type — are also much in evidence in Eastern kitchens. Another essential kitchen item is a pestle and mortar for grinding spices, nuts, chillies etc. because many of the ingredients used are ground before cooking.

Try to get fresh ingredients whenever these are specified in a recipe but, if this is not possible, substitute ground or preserved ginger, tinned bamboo shoots or whatever. You will, though, have to experiment with the quantities involved in such instances because the taste is likely to differ slightly.

Nowadays it is much easier to buy the spices and flavourings needed and many areas have supermarkets or food stores that specialize in such items. Basically, though, Oriental cookery is a simple art: the secret of success lies not so much with the ingredients as with the method of preparation, cooking and presentation . . . enjoy it!

1.

SOUPS

CORN SOUP

Imperial (Metric)
2 dessertspoonsful vegetable oil
1 clove garlic, chopped
Sea salt and freshly ground black
   pepper to taste
1 pint (570ml) water
1 small tin creamed sweet corn
Finely chopped coriander leaves or
   parsley to garnish

American
4 teaspoonsful vegetable oil
1 clove garlic, chopped
Sea salt and freshly ground black
   pepper to taste
2½ cupsful water
1 small can creamed sweet corn
Finely chopped cilantro or parsley to
   garnish

1. Heat oil in pan and brown the garlic. Add salt, pepper and the water. Cover the pan and leave to simmer for 30 minutes.

2. Remove lid from pan, add the creamed sweet corn and serve in individual, heated soup bowls garnished with chopped coriander leaves (cilantro) or parsley.

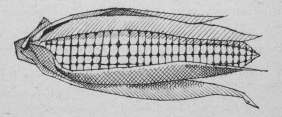

HOT AND SOUR SOUP

Imperial (Metric)	American
2 large dried mushrooms	2 large dried mushrooms
6 cloud ears	6 cloud ears
4 dried tiger-lily stems	4 dried tiger-lily stems
1 tablespoonful vegetable oil	1 tablespoonful vegetable oil
4 oz (115g) bamboo shoots, shredded	4 ounces bamboo shoots, shredded
1 pint (570ml) vegetable stock	2½ cupsful vegetable stock
¼ teaspoonful sea salt	¼ teaspoonful sea salt
2 tablespoonsful wine vinegar	2 tablespoonsful wine vinegar
1 tablespoonful soya sauce	1 tablespoonful soy sauce
1 tablespoonful cornflour	1 tablespoonful cornstarch
1½ tablespoonsful water	1½ tablespoonsful water
½ lb (225g) white bean curd, shredded	8 ounces white bean curd, shredded
1 tablespoonful sesame oil	1 tablespoonful sesame oil
1 teaspoonful freshly ground black pepper	1 teaspoonful freshly ground black pepper
1 egg, lightly beaten	1 egg, lightly beaten
4 finely chopped spring onions for garnish	4 finely chopped scallions for garnish

1. Place dried mushrooms, cloud ears and tiger-lily stems in small basin, pour boiling water over them and then leave to stand for 20-25 minutes.

2. Drain the dried ingredients, discard the mushroom stems and harder parts of the cloud ears; cut into thin slices. Shred the tiger-lily stems using your fingers and, if very long, cut the stems in half.

3. Heat the oil in a pan, add mushrooms, cloud ears and tiger-lily stems. After a minute or two, add the shredded bamboo shoots and the vegetable stock, stirring gently.

4. Add salt, vinegar and soya sauce, stirring gently. Reduce heat and leave to simmer for about 15 minutes.

5. Mix cornflour to a smooth paste with the water and then add this to the simmering broth. Stir the broth and, when it begins to thicken, add the shredded bean curd. Bring to the boil.

6. Turn off heat and leave soup to cool slightly for about 30 seconds before adding the sesame oil and pepper. Stir gently to blend the oil into the mixture.

7. Pour the soup into a hot tureen and gradually add the beaten egg in a thin stream, stirring gently with a circular motion.

8. Sprinkle with chopped spring onions (scallions) and serve immediately.

NOODLE AND WATER CHESTNUT SOUP

Imperial (Metric)	American
3 oz (75g) dried transparent noodles	3 ounces dried transparent noodles
1 pint (570ml) vegetable stock or water	2½ cupsful vegetable stock or water
2 teaspoonsful light soya sauce	2 teaspoonsful light soy sauce
¼ teaspoonful sea salt	¼ teaspoonful sea salt
2 tablespoonsful *sake* or rice wine	2 tablespoonsful *sake* or rice wine
1 small tin water chestnuts	1 small can water chestnuts
Finely chopped spring onion to garnish	Finely chopped scallion to garnish

1. Bring salted water to the boil in a large pan, drop in noodles, boil for 7 minutes, drain, wash in colander under running cold water, drain and set aside.

2. Bring vegetable stock to the boil in a large pan; add soya sauce, salt and *sake*. Reduce heat and leave to simmer for 5-8 minutes.

3. Drain water chestnuts, cut into thin slices and add to soup.

4. Cut noodles into 2 in. (5cm) lengths, drop into soup, allow to simmer for further 2-3 minutes and serve in individual, heated soup bowls garnished with chopped spring onion (scallion).

SANTAN SOUP (SOTHI)

Imperial (Metric)
3 small red onions
2 red and 2 green chillies
1 tablespoonful coconut oil
¼ teaspoonful anise, ground
¼ teaspoonful mustard seeds,
  ground
2 curry leaves, washed
¼ pint (140ml) thin santan
  (page 109)
¼ teaspoonful turmeric powder
1 medium potato, peeled and sliced
1 large tomato, sliced
¼ pint (140ml) thick santan
  (page 109)
Juice of ½ lime or lemon

American
3 small red onions
2 red and 2 green chillies
1 tablespoonful coconut oil
¼ teaspoonful anise, ground
¼ teaspoonful mustard seeds,
  ground
2 curry leaves, washed
⅔ cupful thin santan (page 109)
¼ teaspoonful turmeric powder
1 medium potato, peeled and sliced
1 large tomato, sliced
⅔ cupful thick santan (page 109)
Juice of ½ lime or lemon

1. Peel and slice the onions; wash the chillies, remove the seeds and cut into thin slices.

2. Heat the oil in a pan, add sliced onions and chillies, anise, mustard seeds and curry leaves. Fry together, stirring continuously, until light golden brown.

3. Add the thin santan and turmeric powder, bring very slowly to the boil while stirring continuously and allow to cook for about 10 minutes.

4. Add the sliced potato and tomato; cook at simmering point for about 15 minutes until potato slices are soft.

5. Add thick santan and bring slowly to the boil, stirring continuously, until soup thickens.

6. Remove from heat, add lime juice and serve immediately in heated soup bowls.

MUSHROOM AND NOODLE SOUP

Imperial (Metric)	American
2 oz (55g) cellophane noodles	2 ounces cellophane noodles
20 dried black mushrooms	20 dried black mushrooms
1 pint (570ml) boiling water	2½ cupsful boiling water
Sea salt and freshly ground black pepper to taste	Sea salt and freshly ground black pepper to taste
2 tablespoonsful white wine	2 tablespoonsful white wine
Chopped parsley to garnish	Chopped parsley to garnish

1. Put noodles to soak in warm water for 30 minutes.

2. Place mushrooms in bowl, cover with the boiling water and leave to stand for 20 minutes.

3. Remove soaked mushrooms from liquid (which should be retained), remove their stems and cut in half.

4. Drain soaked noodles, place in a colander, rinse under running cold water and drain again.

5. Pour the retained mushroom liquid through a strainer into a measuring jug and add sufficient cold water to bring the level back to 1 pint (570ml/2½ cupsful).

6. Pour this liquid into a pan, add drained noodles, mushrooms, salt, pepper and wine. Bring to the boil.

7. When boiling, reduce heat, simmer gently for 10 minutes and then serve in individual, heated soup bowls garnished with parsley.

CELESTIAL SOUP

Imperial (Metric)
2 cloves garlic, chopped
1 spring onion, chopped
1 teaspoonful sesame oil
¼ teaspoonful sea salt
1 tablespoonful soya sauce
1 pint (570ml) water

American
2 cloves garlic, chopped
1 scallion, chopped
1 teaspoonful sesame oil
¼ teaspoonful sea salt
1 tablespoonful soy sauce
2½ cupsful water

1. Mix the chopped garlic and onion with the sesame oil, salt and soya sauce.

2. Bring the water to the boil in a pan, add the other ingredients, boil for further minute, strain and serve in individual soup bowls as a drink to cleanse the palate.

TOMATO AND ONION SOUP

Imperial (Metric)	American
2 large tomatoes	2 large tomatoes
1 large onion	1 large onion
3½ tablespoonsful vegetable oil	3½ tablespoonsful vegetable oil
1 pint (570ml) water	2½ cupsful water
1 teaspoonful light soya sauce	1 teaspoonful light soy sauce
½ teaspoonful sea salt	½ teaspoonful sea salt
1 egg, lightly beaten	1 egg, lightly beaten

1. Wash and remove stems from tomatoes; cut into sixths vertically.

2. Peel the onion and cut in the same way as the tomatoes.

3. Heat oil in a pan and lightly fry the tomatoes and onion for about 3-4 minutes.

4. Add the water, bring to the boil, reduce heat and simmer for 5 minutes.

5. Add the soya sauce and salt, stirring gently.

6. Turn up the heat briefly and add the egg, little by little, and serve immediately.

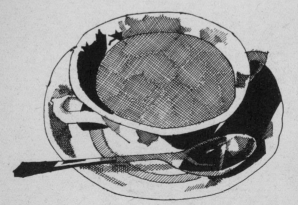

BAMBOO SHOOT AND SEAWEED SOUP

Imperial (Metric)
1 small bamboo shoot, thinly sliced
2 teaspoonsful soya sauce
2 pieces dried lobe-leaf seaweed
  (*wakami*) about 6 in. (15cm) long
1 pint (570ml) vegetable stock or
  water
¼ teaspoonful sea salt

American
1 small bamboo shoot, thinly sliced
2 teaspoonsful soy sauce
2 pieces dried lobe-leaf seaweed
  (*wakami*) about 6 in. long
2½ cupsful vegetable stock or water
¼ teaspoonful sea salt

1. Sprinkle the finely chopped bamboo shoot with soya sauce and leave to stand.

2. Cover the dried seaweed with cold water and leave to soak for 20 minutes until soft.

3. Bring the vegetable stock to the boil in a saucepan. When boiling, reduce heat, add seasoning and bamboo shoots (including the soya sauce), simmer for 5 minutes.

4. Drain the seaweed and cut into short lengths no larger than the bamboo slices. Place a few pieces in individual, heated soup bowls and pour the simmering broth over them.

CHINESE WATERCRESS SOUP

Imperial (Metric)	American
½ lb (225g) Chinese watercress*	8 ounces Chinese watercress*
1 teaspoonful cornflour	1 teaspoonful cornstarch
½ teaspoonful raw cane sugar	½ teaspoonful raw cane sugar
½ teaspoonful freshly ground black pepper	½ teaspoonful freshly ground black pepper
2 teaspoonsful soya sauce	2 teaspoonsful soy sauce
1 tablespoonful sesame oil	1 tablespoonful sesame oil
1 slice fresh ginger, shredded	1 slice fresh ginger, shredded
½ teaspoonful sea salt	½ teaspoonful sea salt
1 pint (570ml) boiling water	2½ cupsful boiling water
2 eggs, lightly beaten	2 eggs, lightly beaten

1. Rinse the watercress and trim off any unsightly or woody stems; leave to drain.

2. Mix the cornflour, sugar, pepper and soya sauce to a paste with a little of the oil.

3. Heat the remainder of the oil in a pan, add the shredded ginger and salt, fry gently for a few seconds, stirring with a wooden spoon, then add the boiling water.

4. Bring to a fresh boil, toss in the watercress, cover with a lid and simmer for 10 minutes.

5. Add the paste ingredients, replace the lid and boil for 6 minutes.

6. Remove from flame and leave (still covered) for 3 minutes.

7. Carefully pour the beaten eggs into the hot soup in a thin stream, stirring gently. Serve immediately in individual, heated soup bowls.

*Finely shredded cabbage can be substituted for watercress.

DRIED MUSHROOM AND BEAN CURD SOUP

Imperial (Metric)
4 large dried mushrooms
1 pint (570ml) vegetable stock or
  water
½ lb (225g) white bean curd
Sea salt and freshly ground black
  pepper to taste

American
4 large dried mushrooms
2½ cupsful vegetable stock or water
8 ounces white bean curd
Sea salt and freshly ground black
  pepper to taste

1. Wash mushrooms then leave to soak for 15 minutes in small basin of warm water. Drain, remove stalks and cut into thin slices.

2. Place sliced mushrooms in cold stock, heat to simmering point, allow to simmer for a further 15 minutes.

3. Wash and dry bean curd, cut into small pieces about the same size as mushroom slices.

4. Add bean curd slices to pan and simmer gently for about 10 minutes until bean curd is heated through thoroughly.

5. Add seasoning to taste and serve immediately in heated soup bowls.

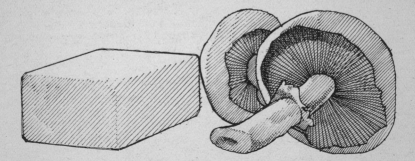

COCONUT SOUP

Imperial (Metric)
½ coconut for santan (page 109)
3 small red onions
2 red chillies
2 green chillies
1 tomato
1 potato
1 tablespoonful coconut oil
½ teaspoonful anise
¼ teaspoonful mustard seeds
2 curry leaves
¼ teaspoonful turmeric powder
Juice of ½ lime or lemon

American
½ coconut for santan (page 109)
3 small red onions
2 red chillies
2 green chillies
1 tomato
1 potato
1 tablespoonful coconut oil
½ teaspoonful anise
¼ teaspoonful mustard seeds
2 curry leaves
¼ teaspoonful turmeric powder
Juice of ½ lime or lemon

1. Scrape coconut and prepare ¼ pint (140ml/⅔ cupful) thick santan and ¼ pint (140ml/⅔ cupful) thin santan.

2. Peel onions and slice thinly.

3. Wash red and green chillies, remove seeds and cut into slices diagonally.

4. Wash tomato, slice and chop small.

5. Wash and peel potato, cut into thick slices.

6. Heat oil, add sliced onions, chillies, anise, mustard seeds and curry leaves. Fry together, stirring all the time, until light brown in colour.

7. Add thin santan and turmeric powder, bring slowly to the boil stirring continuously.

8. Add sliced potato and chopped tomato, allow to simmer for 15-20 minutes until potato is cooked.

9. Add thick santan and bring slowly to boiling point, stirring all the time, until soup thickens.

10. Remove from heat, add lime or lemon juice and serve immediately in warm soup bowls.

EGG SOUP

Imperial (Metric)
1 pint (570ml) vegetable stock or
   water
2 eggs
2 teaspoonsful light soya sauce
Sea salt and freshly ground black
   pepper to taste
1 spring onion for garnish

American
2½ cupsful vegetable stock or water
2 eggs
2 teaspoonsful light soy sauce
Sea salt and freshly ground black
   pepper to taste
1 scallion for garnish

1. Heat stock or water to simmering point.

2. Lightly beat the eggs in a bowl with salt and pepper.

3. Pour lightly beaten egg as a continuous thread into the simmering liquid, stirring all the time.

4. Add soya sauce and simmer gently for about 3 minutes until the egg is just set.

5. Serve immediately in heated soup bowls and garnish with finely chopped spring onion (scallion).

WALNUT DATE SOUP

Like many Chinese soups, this is served at the end of a meal as a dessert.

Imperial (Metric)
About 20 dried Chinese dates
2 pints (1.15 litres) water
½ lb (225g) shelled walnuts
2 oz (55g) raw cane sugar
2 teaspoonsful cornflour

American
About 20 dried Chinese dates
5 cupsful water
1¾ cupsful shelled English walnuts
⅓ cupful raw cane sugar
2 teaspoonsful cornstarch

1. Soak the dried dates in half the cold water for 4 hours. Drain.

2. Put the rest of the water in a saucepan, add the dates and bring to the boil. When boiling, reduce heat, cover and simmer for 1½-2 hours. Allow the dates to cool, drain off the liquid but retain it for later use.

3. Peel and stone the dates, set aside.

4. In a pan boil enough water to cover the walnuts. When boiling, add the shelled walnuts and simmer for 5 minutes; drain.

5. Blend the date pulp and walnuts together with half the reserved date liquid until the mixture is smooth. (This can most easily be achieved by using an electric blender; if done manually, the walnuts will have to be pounded lightly in a mortar.)

6. Pour the mixture into a saucepan, add the rest of the reserved date liquid, stir in the sugar and bring to the boil slowly, continuing to stir.

7. Blend the cornflour to a smooth paste with 1 tablespoonful of cold water. Reduce the heat under the saucepan, add the cornflour and simmer for 3-4 minutes, stirring continuously. Serve hot.

2.

MAIN DISHES

Stir-frying

In Far Eastern countries the most usual method of cooking vegetables is to stir-fry them in order to retain their natural flavour and colour. In the West there is a tendency to overcook vegetables so that they become soggy, and to throw away the water in which they are cooked — along with all those health-giving vitamins.

Although Western palates may take a while to adjust to what may be regarded as undercooked vegetables, once one has savoured the real taste of crisp, green cabbage as opposed to the glutinous mess that is served in most Western restaurants, even a simple dish of unadorned vegetable takes on new dimensions.

Here, then, is the basic method for stir-frying vegetables:

1. Put a small quantity of oil into a wok or frying-pan and when the oil is moderately hot add the vegetable to be cooked. Stir in order to ensure that every part of the vegetable has been coated in oil.

2. Cover the pan with a lid to avoid excessive splashing and cook for not more than 3 minutes.

3. Remove the cover from the pan and continue cooking for a further minute or two, adding a little water if cooking beans, peas, mushrooms, bean sprouts, bamboo shoots and the like but not if cooking leafy vegetables such as spinach, cabbage or watercress, as these contain sufficient water already.

Try to avoid the temptation to cook any longer than this (unless specified otherwise in a particular recipe) because it really isn't necessary, especially if one bears in mind that vegetables are nearly always cut into pieces small enough to be picked up easily with chopsticks. A little salt is used for seasoning and is fried lightly in the oil before adding the vegetable that is to be cooked.

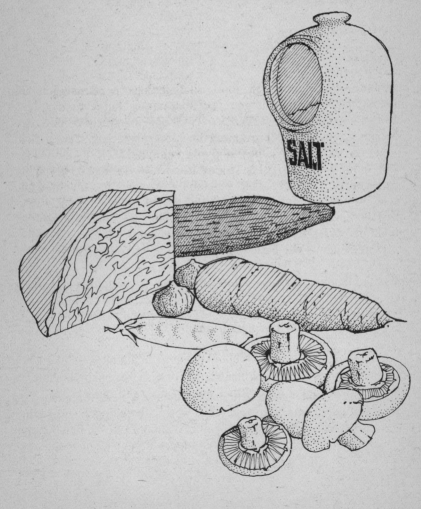

MIXED FRIED VEGETABLES I

Imperial (Metric)	American
½ lb (225g) round cabbage	8 ounces round cabbage
6 dried mushrooms	6 dried mushrooms
4 oz (100g) bamboo shoots	4 ounces bamboo shoots
2 oz (55g) mangetout peas	2 ounces snow peas
1 carrot	1 carrot
1 small cucumber	1 small cucumber
4 oz (115g) water chestnuts	4 ounces water chestnuts
5 tablespoonsful oil	5 tablespoonsful oil
1 teaspoonful sea salt	1 teaspoonful sea salt
1 tablespoonful raw cane sugar	1 tablespoonful raw cane sugar
2 teaspoonsful soya sauce	2 teaspoonsful soy sauce
5 tablespoonsful vegetable stock	5 tablespoonsful vegetable stock

1. Wash and prepare the vegetables. Core and trim the cabbage, cut into 1 in. (2.5cm) pieces; soak the dried mushrooms until soft, drain, remove their stems and cut them in half; cut the bamboo shoots into thin strips; string, but do not shell, the mangetout (snow) peas, cook in salted boiling water for 5 minutes; slice the carrot and cook in salted boiling water for 5 minutes; slice the cucumber diagonally, discard the two end pieces; peel and slice the water chestnuts.

2. Heat the oil and fry the cabbage over a high heat for 2-3 minutes.

3. Reduce the heat, add all the other vegetables and continue to fry for 5 minutes, stirring occasionally.

4. Add seasoning and stock, mix well.

5. Serve immediately on a heated plate or dish. Or, as this is a fairly light dish, leave to cool in a serving dish and serve cold.

FRIED MIXED VEGETABLES II

Imperial (Metric)	American
2 oz (55g) carrots	2 ounces carrots
2 small courgettes	2 small zucchini
4 oz (115g) cauliflower florets	4 ounces cauliflower florets
2 oz (55g) button mushrooms	2 ounces button mushrooms
1 stick celery	1 stalk celery
Vegetable oil for deep-frying	Vegetable oil for deep-frying
4 tablespoonsful soya sauce	4 tablespoonsful soy sauce
2 tablespoonsful raw cane sugar	2 tablespoonsful raw cane sugar
1 pint (570ml) vegetable stock	2½ cupsful vegetable stock
2 tablespoonsful red wine	2 tablespoonsful red wine
2 oz (55g) tinned sweetcorn kernels, drained	⅓ cupful tinned sweetcorn kernels, drained
2 oz (55g) shelled cashew nuts	½ cupful shelled cashew nuts
2 oz (55g) fresh shelled or frozen peas	½ cupful fresh shelled or frozen peas
1 teaspoonful cornflour mixed to a paste with 1 tablespoonful cold water	1 teaspoonful cornstarch mixed to a paste with 1 tablespoonful cold water

1. Wash and drain the carrots, cauliflower, courgettes (zucchini), mushrooms and celery.

2. Cook the carrots in salted boiling water for 5 minutes until soft; drain and slice, discarding the end pieces. Cut the courgettes (zucchini) into slices about ½ in. (1.25cm) thick; break the cauliflower into small pieces; slice the celery and halve the mushrooms.

3. Deep-fry the courgettes (zucchini) in hot oil for 3-4 minutes until tender; remove and leave to drain. Place the carrots, cauliflower, mushrooms and celery in the hot oil and cook for 3-4 minutes; remove and drain.

4. Pour the oil out of the pan, return the above ingredients to it and cook briefly over a high heat.

5. Mix the soya sauce, sugar, stock and wine together in a bowl or
    jug, then pour this mixture over the vegetables in the pan. Add
    the sweetcorn, cashews and peas; simmer for 15 minutes.

6. Add the thickening, simmer for a further 2-3 minutes, stirring
    gently. Serve hot.

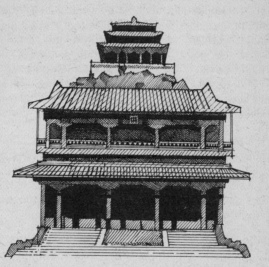

RUNNER BEANS IN SAVOURY SAUCE

Imperial (Metric)	American
2 candle nuts	2 candle nuts
6 small red onions	6 small red onions
3 fresh chillies, seeded	3 fresh chillies, seeded
1 teaspoonful crunchy peanut butter	1 teaspoonful crunchy peanut butter
1½ tablespoonsful vegetable oil	1½ tablespoonsful vegetable oil
½ pint (285ml) thin santan (page 109)	1⅓ cupsful thin santan (page 109)
1 lb (455g) runner beans	1 pound green beans
1 lb (455g) yellow bean curd	1 pound yellow bean curd
¼ teaspoonful sea salt	¼ teaspoonful sea salt
½ pint (285ml) thick santan (page 109)	1⅓ cupsful thick santan (page 109)

1. Chop the candle nuts and onions, put into mortar with seeded chillies and peanut butter and grind to a smooth paste.

2. Heat the oil in a pan, add ground ingredients and cook until onions are golden brown. Add thin santan and simmer.

3. Wash and string the runner beans, cut the bean curd into small squares and add both to the other ingredients in the pan with the salt. Continue to cook until the beans are tender.

4. When the beans are cooked, add the thick santan and simmer, stirring occasionally, until boiling point is reached. Serve with rice or noodles.

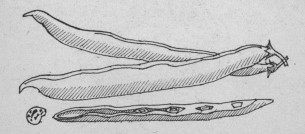

SAUTÉED CABBAGE

Imperial (Metric)	American
1 lb (455g) round cabbage	1 pound round cabbage
4 tablespoonsful vegetable oil	4 tablespoonsful vegetable oil
1 clove garlic, crushed	1 clove garlic, crushed
3 red peppers, chopped	3 red peppers, chopped
1 tablespoonful soya sauce	1 tablespoonful soy sauce
2 tablespoonsful cider vinegar	2 tablespoonsful cider vinegar
2 tablespoonsful raw cane sugar	2 tablespoonsful raw cane sugar
½ teaspoonful sea salt	½ teaspoonful sea salt
1 teaspoonful cornflour	1 teaspoonful cornstarch
2 teaspoonsful water	2 teaspoonsful water

1. Wash cabbage and cut into triangular pieces about 2 in. (5cm) thick.

2. Heat oil, add crushed garlic and chopped red peppers, fry for 2 or 3 minutes.

3. Add cabbage and fry over a strong flame, stirring constantly.

4. Add sugar, vinegar, soya sauce and salt. Continue to stir over a high flame for further 2 or 3 minutes.

5. Mix cornflour to smooth paste with the water and add to fried ingredients. Cook, still stirring, until the mixture has thickened. Serve hot.

BRAISED BAMBOO SHOOTS WITH MUSHROOMS AND BEANS

Imperial (Metric)	American
½ lb (225g) tin of bamboo shoots	8 ounce can of bamboo shoots
½ lb (225g) shelled butter beans	8 ounces shelled Lima beans
8 large dried mushrooms	8 large dried mushrooms
5 tablespoonsful vegetable oil	5 tablespoonsful vegetable oil
1 tablespoonful wine	1 tablespoonful wine
4 tablespoonsful soya sauce	4 tablespoonsful soy sauce
2 tablespoonsful raw cane sugar	2 tablespoonsful raw cane sugar
6 tablespoonsful water	6 tablespoonsful water

1. Prepare vegetables as follows: cut bamboo shoots into cubes; soak mushrooms in hot water for 10 minutes, drain, remove stems and halve; remove skins from beans.

2. Heat oil and fry bamboo shoots, mushrooms and beans.

3. Add all other ingredients, cover with lid and simmer for about 20 minutes until all liquid has been absorbed. Serve hot.

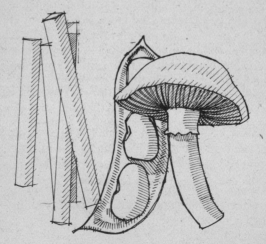

SAUTÉED PINEAPPLE AND VEGETABLE CUBES

Imperial (Metric)	American
4 oz (115g) carrots	4 ounces carrots
2 potatoes	2 potatoes
2 thick slices wholemeal bread	2 thick slices wholewheat bread
1 large onion	1 large onion
1 green pepper	1 green pepper
2 oz (55g) mangetout peas	2 ounces snow peas
Vegetable oil for deep-frying	Vegetable oil for deep-frying
2 cloves garlic, crushed	2 cloves garlic, crushed
1 tablespoonful soya sauce	1 tablespoonful soy sauce
½ teaspoonful sea salt	½ teaspoonful sea salt
1 tablespoonful cornflour	1 tablespoonful cornstarch
5 tablespoonsful water	5 tablespoonsful water
Small tin pineapple cubes, drained	Small can pineapple cubes, drained

1. Wash, scrape and dice carrots into ½ in. (1.25cm) cubes. Cook in salted boiling water for about 5 minutes until soft; drain.

2. Wash and peel potatoes; cut into small cubes. Remove crusts from the bread and cut into cubes. Peel and dice the onion; wash and de-seed the pepper, cut into ½ in. (1.25cm) squares. Wash and string the peas but do not remove their shells, cut into ½ in. lengths.

3. Heat oil for deep-frying and cook the potato and bread cubes separately until crisp and golden brown. Drain the cubes, set aside and pour most of the oil out of the pan.

4. Reheat the pan and sauté the garlic, onion, green pepper, potatoes, carrots and peas over a high heat for 3-4 minutes. Reduce the heat and add the soya sauce, salt, and cornflour mixed to a paste with the cold water. Bring to the boil.

5. Add the bread cubes and drained pineapple, stir in well and serve immediately.

TURNIPS WITH BEAN STUFFING

Imperial (Metric)	American
4 medium turnips	4 medium turnips
6 in. (15cm) length of dried kelp	6 in. length of dried kelp
½ pint (285ml) vegetable stock	1⅓ cupsful vegetable stock
1 tablespoonful raw cane sugar	1 tablespoonful raw cane sugar
1 tablespoonful soya sauce	1 tablespoonful soy sauce
½ teaspoonful sea salt	½ teaspoonful sea salt

Stuffing:

Imperial (Metric)	American
½ lb (225g) red bean paste	8 ounces red bean paste
1 tablespoonful raw cane sugar	1 tablespoonful raw cane sugar
3 tablespoonsful rice wine	3 tablespoonsful rice wine
1½ tablespoonsful vegetable stock	1½ tablespoonsful vegetable stock
1 egg yolk	1 egg yolk
Grated rind of ½ lemon	Grated rind of ½ lemon

1. Wash the turnips thoroughly, top and tail them but otherwise leave whole.

2. Parboil the turnips for 8 minutes in a saucepan of salted boiling water; remove from the pan, rinse under cold water and drain.

3. Put the kelp in a saucepan with the vegetable stock, bring to the boil and remove the kelp.

4. Add the sugar, soya sauce and salt to the kelp-flavoured stock. Drop in the turnips, bring to the boil and continue to cook until the turnips are tender. Set aside in a warm place.

5. Mix all of the stuffing ingredients together until smooth, place in the top of a double boiler and cook for about 7 or 8 minutes until the mixture begins to thicken.

6. Drain the turnips, reserving some stock, cut off their tops and scoop out a hollow in the centre of each. Fill these hollows with the bean stuffing, replace the turnip tops, place on a heated serving dish and pour any surplus stuffing (thinned, if necessary, with a drop of the stock) over them. Serve hot.

GRILLED LEEKS WITH BEAN PASTE

Imperial (Metric)	American
6 leeks	6 leeks
2 tablespoonsful vegetable oil	2 tablespoonsful vegetable oil
2 tablespoonsful raw cane sugar	2 tablespoonsful raw cane sugar
2 tablespoonsful vegetable stock	2 tablespoonsful vegetable stock
2 tablespoonsful rice wine	2 tablespoonsful rice wine
4 tablespoonsful red bean paste	4 tablespoonsful red bean paste

1. Wash the leeks, discard the root ends and cut into 1½ in. (4cm) lengths.

2. Brush the pieces of leek with oil and grill until soft (this is probably easiest if the leek sections are skewered before placing under the grill).

3. Meanwhile mix all the other ingredients together in a bowl.

4. When the leeks are cooked, brush liberally with the bean paste mixture and return to the grill. Cook under a low heat until the paste is dry and has formed a glaze.

5. Serve immediately, utilizing any sauce that has accumulated in the bottom of the grill pan by pouring this over the cooked leeks.

SPINACH WITH PEANUTS

Imperial (Metric)	American
1 lb (455g) spinach	1 pound spinach
½ lb (225g) shelled peanuts	1½ cupsful shelled peanuts
2½ tablespoonsful soya sauce	2½ tablespoonsful soy sauce

1. Wash the spinach thoroughly and cut off any tough stems. Tie the spinach together with a length of twine or raffia so that the stems lie together and the whole thing forms a long, narrow cylinder.

2. Bring a large saucepan of salted water to the boil, add the spinach and push it below the water level with a wooden spoon. Bring the water back to the boil and cook the spinach for a further 3 minutes.

3. Remove the spinach from the saucepan and plunge it immediately into a bowl of iced water; drain well by squeezing any excess water out by hand without spoiling its shape.

4. Remove the twine and cut the spinach into 1 in. (2.5cm) lengths. Gently mix these segments with half the soya sauce and place neatly on a serving dish.

5. Dry roast the peanuts over a low heat for 5-10 minutes, stirring occasionally with a spatula to ensure that they do not burn. Remove from the pan and grind coarsely in a mortar.

6. Mix the ground peanuts with the remainder of the soya sauce and pour this mixture over the spinach rolls. Serve hot or cold.

AUBERGINE CURRY

Imperial (Metric)
2 lb (900g) aubergines
2 tablespoonsful vegetable oil
1 teaspoonful ground turmeric
1 teaspoonful cumin seeds, ground
6 whole peppercorns
4 cloves
1 teaspoonful coriander seeds
1/2 teaspoonful anise seeds
4 medium tomatoes, skinned and
  chopped
Small piece fresh ginger, shredded
4 green chillies, seeded and finely
  chopped
1/2 teaspoonful sea salt
Juice of 1 lime or lemon
1/4 pint (140ml) warm water
Chopped coriander leaves or parsley
  to garnish

American
2 pounds eggplants
2 tablespoonsful vegetable oil
1 teaspoonful ground turmeric
1 teaspoonful cumin seeds, ground
6 whole peppercorns
4 cloves
1 teaspoonful coriander seeds
1/2 teaspoonful anise seeds
4 medium tomatoes, skinned and
  chopped
Small piece fresh ginger, shredded
4 green chillies, seeded and finely
  chopped
1/2 teaspoonful sea salt
Juice of 1 lime or lemon
2/3 cupful warm water
Chopped cilantro or parsley to
  garnish

1. Wash and peel the aubergines (eggplants); cut into quarters, sixths or eighths according to size and cover with cold water to avoid discolouration.

2. Heat the oil to haze heat, add the turmeric, cumin, peppercorns, cloves, coriander seeds and anise seeds. Cook for 3-4 minutes, stirring constantly.

3. Add the tomatoes, ginger, chillies and salt; reduce heat and cook for 8-10 minutes, stirring occasionally.

4. Add the aubergines (eggplants) and lime juice, cover the pan and cook over low heat for 10 minutes. Add warm water, replace the lid and simmer for about 10 minutes until the aubergines (eggplants) are tender.

5. Serve garnished with coriander leaves (cilantro) or parsley.

SPICED POTATOES

Imperial (Metric)	American
1 lb (455g) medium potatoes	1 pound medium potatoes
1 teaspoonful turmeric powder	1 teaspoonful turmeric powder
2 teaspoonsful sea salt	2 teaspoonsful sea salt
2 teaspoonsful cumin seeds	2 teaspoonsful cumin seeds
1 large onion, peeled and diced	1 large onion, peeled and diced
1 teaspoonful fresh ginger, shredded	1 teaspoonful fresh ginger, shredded
2 red chillies, ground to smooth paste	2 red chillies, ground to smooth paste
¼ pint (140ml) water	⅔ cupful water
Vegetable oil for cooking	Vegetable oil for cooking
1 teaspoonful coriander seeds	1 teaspoonful coriander seeds
1 teaspoonful anise	1 teaspoonful anise
1 teaspoonful poppy seeds	1 teaspoonful poppy seeds

1. Wash and peel potatoes. Cut into eighths by quartering lengthwise then halving each piece.

2. Place potato pieces in a dish, add turmeric powder, salt and 1 teaspoonful cumin seeds. Leave for 15 minutes then drain in a colander.

3. Heat oil in a pan and fry the potatoes in batches until golden brown, drain and remove to a plate.

4. Put 2 tablespoonsful of the oil used for frying the potatoes in a pan and cook the diced onion until it is soft but not browned.

5. Add the shredded ginger and ground chillies. Stir for a few seconds then add the water and bring to the boil slowly.

6. When boiling, add the fried potatoes and cook slowly, stirring occasionally, until all the liquid has been absorbed.

7. Meanwhile, roast the remaining ingredients for a few seconds in a dry pan to bring out their aroma then pound them in a mortar until coarsely ground.

8. Stir the pounded spices into the potatoes just before serving.

GRILLED AUBERGINES WITH SESAME SEEDS

Imperial (Metric)	American
2 medium aubergines	2 medium eggplants
Sea salt	Sea salt
2 tablespoonsful white sesame seeds	2 tablespoonsful white sesame seeds
4 spring onions, finely chopped	4 scallions, finely chopped
¼ teaspoonful ground red pepper	¼ teaspoonful ground red pepper
2 tablespoonsful soya sauce	2 tablespoonsful soy sauce
1 teaspoonful raw cane sugar	1 teaspoonful raw cane sugar

1. Wash but do not peel the aubergines (eggplants), cut into slices about 1 in. (2.5cm) thick, place on a large plate, sprinkle with salt and leave for 30 minutes.

2. Toast the sesame seeds in a dry pan until they start jumping. Remove from the heat and grind in a mortar.

3. When the aubergines (eggplants) have been standing for half an hour, drain away any excess liquid and pat dry with a clean cloth or absorbent paper. Grill slowly until tender.

4. Prepare the spicy sauce while the aubergines (eggplants) are cooking. Put ground sesame seeds, chopped onions, red pepper, soya sauce and sugar in a small saucepan and heat gently, stirring occasionally, until heated thoroughly.

5. Arrange the grilled aubergines (eggplants) on a heated serving dish, sprinkle with the spice mixture and serve immediately.

GREEN PEPPERS STUFFED WITH CARROTS

Imperial (Metric)	American
8 medium green peppers	8 medium green peppers
2 lb (900g) carrots	2 pounds carrots
2 large onions	2 large onions
4 tablespoonsful vegetable oil	4 tablespoonsful vegetable oil
4 tablespoonsful tomato ketchup	4 tablespoonsful tomato catsup
1 tablespoonful raw cane sugar	1 tablespoonful raw cane sugar
1 teaspoonful sea salt	1 teaspoonful sea salt
Freshly ground black pepper	Freshly ground black pepper
½ pint (285ml) water	1⅓ cupsful water

1. Parboil the green peppers, rinse in cold water and drain. Cut off their tops and remove the seeds.

2. Wash and remove tops of the carrots; shred.

3. Peel the onions and cut into very fine slices.

4. Heat oil in a pan and sauté the shredded carrots and onions. Add ketchup, sugar and seasonings.

5. Stuff the peppers with the seasoned carrot mixture; stand them in a large pan, add the water, cover and simmer gently for about 20 minutes until the peppers are tender. Serve hot.

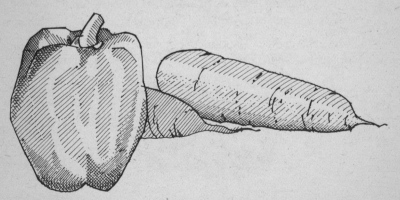

SWEET POTATOES WITH CHESTNUTS

Imperial (Metric)	American
¾ lb (340g) sweet potatoes	12 ounces sweet potatoes
½ lb (225g) raw cane sugar	8 ounces raw cane sugar
3 tablespoonsful white wine	3 tablespoonsful white wine
10-12 tinned chestnuts	10-12 canned chestnuts

1. Peel the potatoes and cut into 1 in. (2.5cm) cubes. Cook in boiling water until tender, drain and mash immediately.

2. Add half the sugar to the mashed sweet potato and stir vigorously until the mixture is quite smooth.

3. Pour the wine into a large saucepan and boil until it has been reduced to about half its volume. Add the rest of the sugar to the wine in the pan and simmer until the sugar has dissolved.

4. Add the mashed sweet potato and continue to cook slowly over a low flame, stirring gently, until the mixture has the consistency of jam.

5. Drain the chestnuts, cut into quarters and mix into the potato mixture just before serving.

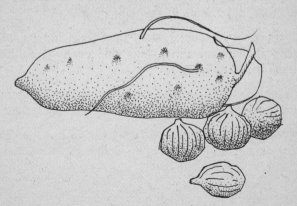

VEGETABLE SOTHI

Imperial (Metric)

½ pint (275ml) thin santan
   (page 109)
1¼ teaspoonsful turmeric powder
2 sprigs curry leaves
2 large onions
¼ teaspoonful sea salt
2 large potatoes
¼ lb (115g) round cabbage
¼ lb (115g) French beans
¼ lb (115g) okra (ladies' fingers)
¼ lb (115g) carrots
3 red and 3 green chillies
½ pint (285ml) thick santan
   (page 109)
Juice of 1 lime or lemon

American

1⅓ cupsful thin santan (page 109)
1¼ teaspoonsful turmeric powder
2 sprigs curry leaves
2 large onions
¼ teaspoonful sea salt
2 large potatoes
4 ounces round cabbage
4 ounces snap beans
4 ounces okra (ladies' fingers)
4 ounces carrots
3 red and 3 green chillies
1⅓ cupsful thick santan (page 109)
Juice of 1 lime or lemon

1. Put thin santan, turmeric and curry leaves in a large saucepan and bring slowly to the boil.

2. Peel the onions, cut into wedges and add to the saucepan.

3. Peel the potatoes, cut into chunks and add these, with the salt, to the other ingredients in the pan; simmer.

4. Wash the other vegetables; string the beans and cut into thick slices; cut the cabbage into chunks and coarsely slice the chillies, but leave the okra whole.

5. When the potatoes are half-cooked, add all the other vegetables to the pan and continue to simmer until all are tender.

6. Slowly add the thick santan, stirring gently to avoid curdling and, when the gravy boils, remove pan from heat, add lime or lemon juice and serve hot with curry.

BAMBOO SHOOTS WITH CHILLI SAUCE

Imperial (Metric)	American
2 lb (900g) fresh bamboo shoots	2 pounds fresh bamboo shoots
Vegetable oil for deep-frying	Vegetable oil for deep-frying
3 tablespoonsful sesame oil	3 tablespoonsful sesame oil
2 tablespoonsful chilli sauce	2 tablespoonsful chilli sauce
1 tablespoonful soya sauce	1 tablespoonful soy sauce
1 teaspoonful raw cane sugar	1 teaspoonful raw cane sugar

1. Boil the bamboo shoots for 25 minutes in salted water, drain, cut into thin slices diagonally.

2. Heat oil for deep-frying and fry the bamboo shoots until golden brown; drain and set aside.

3. Heat the sesame oil in a pan, add the chilli sauce and, when the mixture is hot, add the bamboo shoots, soya sauce and sugar.

4. Cook for 5 minutes, stirring gently, then spoon the ingredients onto a heated serving dish and serve immediately.

TEMPURA

Tempura is probably the best-known Japanese dish in the West. Basically, it usually consists of pieces of fish and vegetables dipped in batter and deep-fried in oil, yet it bears little resemblance to the thickly battered, indigestible offerings usually encountered in Western eateries.

The secret of good tempura lies in the preparation of the batter and the freshness of the ingredients; it is also essential that the tempura should be eaten within seconds of it emerging from the pan, so it is important to make sure that the rice and/or sauces to accompany the tempura are already on the table. Only use fresh, good quality oil and vegetables for tempura and mix the batter immediately before use, never let it 'stand'.

Batter:

Imperial (Metric)	American
1 egg	1 egg
¼ pint (140ml) ice-cold water	⅔ cupful ice-cold water
½ lb (225g) wholemeal flour	2 cupsful wholewheat flour
1 oz (30g) cornflour	2½ tablespoonsful cornstarch

1. Break the egg into a bowl, beat well. Add the water and beat thoroughly until the mixture is very light.

2. Mix the flour and cornflour together and sift it into the bowl containing the egg mixture. Cut the mixture with a fork, do not overmix: it does not matter if the batter is a bit lumpy as long as it is light. If necessary, more water can be added gradually if the batter is too sticky; it should only coat the vegetables thinly.

To Fry:

The pieces of vegetable (absolutely any vegetables can be used as long as they are fresh and cut into small pieces or slices before being dipped in the batter) are dipped quickly into the batter mixture and then deep-fried in very hot oil. If possible, sesame oil is the best oil to use as its slightly nutty flavour enhances the tempura. Test the temperature of the oil by dropping tiny amounts of batter into the oil; if these sink half-way to the bottom of the pan and scatter rapidly, the temperature is right.

Do not fry too many pieces of vegetable at one time as this will cause the temperature of the oil to drop too low. Cook a few pieces of vegetable at a time and, when golden brown, remove to a rack covered with absorbent paper for a second or two, then serve immediately on to a heated plate or into individual bowls placed before each guest.

Tempura is usually accompanied by plain boiled or steamed rice and each tempura portion is dipped into salt or into a special sauce called *Tentsuyu* before eating it while still piping hot.

TENTSUYU SAUCE

Imperial (Metric)
½ pint (285ml) vegetable stock
2 tablespoonsful soya sauce
6 in. (15cm) piece of daikon radish

American
1⅓ cupsful vegetable stock
2 tablespoonsful soy sauce
6 in. piece of daikon radish

1. Put the stock and soya sauce in a saucepan, bring to the boil, remove from the heat but keep warm.

2. Grate the daikon. Pour a little of the warm sauce into several small sauce bowls, place a small heap of daikon in the centre of each and place a sauce bowl in front of each guest.

Note: Lemon juice, mustard, grated ginger or *sake* can be added to this sauce if desired.

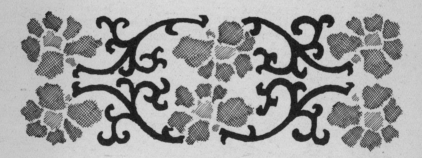

CABBAGE WITH MUSHROOMS

Imperial (Metric)	American
½ lb (225g) fresh mushrooms	8 ounces fresh mushrooms
½ lb (225g) round cabbage	8 ounces round cabbage
3 fl oz (90ml) vegetable oil	⅓ cupful vegetable oil
2 teaspoonsful sea salt	2 teaspoonsful sea salt
1 teaspoonful raw cane sugar	1 teaspoonful raw cane sugar
1 teaspoonful wine (optional)	1 teaspoonful wine (optional)

1. Wash the mushrooms, slice vertically and leave to soak in salted water for about 20 minutes.

2. Wash, core and trim the cabbage. Cut into small sections about 2 in. (5cm) square; wash again and drain.

3. Heat the oil in a pan and fry the mushrooms and cabbage until tender. Add the seasonings and wine, mix well and serve hot.

3.

COLD DISHES

SWEET AND SOUR VEGETABLE SALAD

Imperial (Metric)
½ lb (225g) round cabbage (red or white)
3 cucumbers
5 green peppers
3 tablespoonsful vegetable oil
4 tablespoonsful raw cane sugar
2 tablespoonsful soya sauce
3 tablespoonsful cider vinegar
½ teaspoonful sea salt

American
8 ounces round cabbage (red or white)
3 cucumbers
5 green peppers
3 tablespoonsful vegetable oil
4 tablespoonsful raw cane sugar
2 tablespoonsful soy sauce
3 tablespoonsful cider vinegar
½ teaspoonful sea salt

1. Wash and core cabbage, cut into rough squares about 2 in. (5cm) across.

2. Cut cucumbers into quarters lengthwise, then into fours along each length.

3. Quarter and de-seed the green peppers.

4. Heat the oil and fry all the vegetables over a high flame; add seasonings.

5. Remove to serving dish or plate and chill in refrigerator for at least 1 hour before serving.

JAVANESE POTATO SALAD WITH GADOH-GADOH SAUCE

Imperial (Metric)	American
2 large potatoes	2 large potatoes
1 egg	1 egg
¾ lb (340g) yellow bean curd	12 ounces yellow bean curd
1 tablespoonful vegetable oil	1 tablespoonful vegetable oil
¼ cucumber	¼ cucumber
½ yam	½ yam
2 lb (900g) bean sprouts	2 pounds bean sprouts
6 runner beans	6 green beans
¼ Chinese cabbage	¼ Chinese cabbage
Bunch watercress	Bunch watercress
½ pint (285ml) Gadoh-Gadoh Sauce (page 113)	1⅓ cupsful Gadoh-Gadoh Sauce (page 113)

1. Scrub potatoes and boil in pan of cold water until soft when tested with a fork (about 20-25 minutes). When cooked, remove skins and cut into thick slices.

2. Hard-boil the egg, shell and slice.

3. Wash and dry the bean curd.

4. Heat oil and fry bean curd at haze heat until golden brown on both sides. Drain, cool and cut into cubes.

5. Wash and peel the cucumber and yam. Cut into slices.

6. Wash, prepare and scald bean sprouts, drain well, place in fridge.

7. Wash and string the beans, cut into pieces about 1 in. (2.5cm) long. Cook in salted, boiling water for about 5 minutes, drain well and leave to cool.

8. Wash cabbage and watercress, leaf by leaf, under running cold water. Cut into 1 in. (2.5cm) pieces, cook in small quantity of fast-boiling, salted water in separate, covered pans. Drain well and leave to cool.

9. To serve, either mix all the prepared vegetables together in bowl, pour Gadoh-Gadoh Sauce over top and decorate with slices of hard-boiled egg, or place vegetables in separate heaps on serving dish, garnish with egg and serve the Gadoh-Gadoh Sauce in separate bowl.

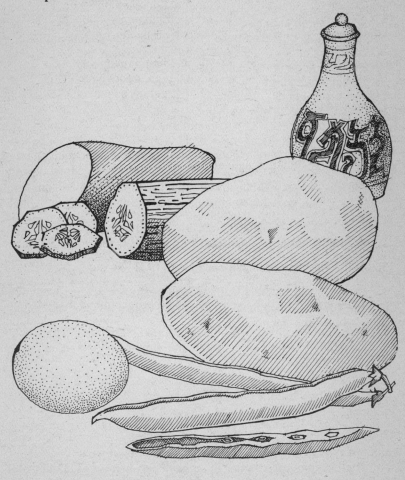

CHINESE PICKLED VEGETABLES

Imperial (Metric)	American
1 lb (455g) red cabbage	1 pound red cabbage
1 large cucumber	1 large cucumber
2 sticks celery	2 stalks celery
1 lb (455g) carrots	1 pound carrots
2 small turnips	2 small turnips
4 thin slices ginger	4 thin slices ginger
4 red peppers, chopped	4 red peppers, chopped
10 black peppercorns	10 black peppercorns
1 tablespoonful sea salt	1 tablespoonful sea salt
1 tablespoonful white wine	1 tablespoonful white wine
3 pints (1.7 litres) water	7½ cupsful water

1. Wash and prepare vegetables: cut cabbage into small pieces; quarter cucumber lengthwise then cut into 2 in. (5cm) lengths; cut celery into 2 in. (5cm) lengths; quarter carrots and cut into 2 in. (5cm) lengths; quarter turnips, then halve again.

2. Wash prepared vegetables again, drain well, mop with clean cloth or kitchen towel and leave to dry thoroughly for at least 4 hours.

3. Bring water to the boil in a large pan, add all seasonings and allow to cool completely.

4. Place all vegetables in large jar or eathenware crock and completely cover with seasoning mixture.

5. Leave to stand for 1 day (summer) or 3 days (winter) before serving.

SWEET AND SOUR CUCUMBERS

Imperial (Metric)	American
8 small cucumbers	8 small cucumbers
2 teaspoonsful sea salt	2 teaspoonsful sea salt
2 teaspoonsful raw cane sugar	2 teaspoonsful raw cane sugar
2 tablespoonsful sesame oil	2 tablespoonsful sesame oil
2 dried mushrooms, soaked	2 dried mushrooms, soaked
2 red peppers	2 red peppers
4 slices ginger	4 slices ginger
2 tablespoonsful raw cane sugar	2 tablespoonsful raw cane sugar
2 tablespoonsful cider vinegar	2 tablespoonsful cider vinegar
1 tablespoonful cornflour	1 tablespoonful cornstarch
5 tablespoonsful water	5 tablespoonsful water

1. Quarter cucumbers lengthwise, then cut each piece into 2 in. (5cm) lengths and remove seeds.

2. Place on plate and sprinkle with salt; allow to stand for 1 hour.

3. Dip cucumbers into pan of boiling water, drain and sprinkle with 2 teaspoonsful sugar.

4. Heat sesame oil in pan and fry shredded mushrooms, shredded red peppers and shredded ginger.

5. Mix 2 tablespoonsful sugar with the vinegar, cornflour and water together to form paste; add to fried ingredients.

6. Mix cucumbers with sauce mixture and chill well before serving.

CHILLED CUCUMBERS AND RADISHES

Imperial (Metric)	American
5 small cucumbers	5 small cucumbers
15 red radishes	15 red radishes
5 tablespoonsful vegetable oil	5 tablespoonsful vegetable oil
3 tablespoonsful cider vinegar	3 tablespoonsful cider vinegar
1 tablespoonful soya sauce	1 tablespoonful soy sauce
1 teaspoonful salt	1 teaspoonful salt
Dash ground garlic	Dash ground garlic

1. Wash cucumbers and cut into thirds, then quarter lengthwise.

2. Wash radishes and crack them open by hitting with back of heavy knife.

3. Heat oil and fry cucumbers and radishes.

4. Add seasonings, stir briskly and remove from heat; chill and serve.

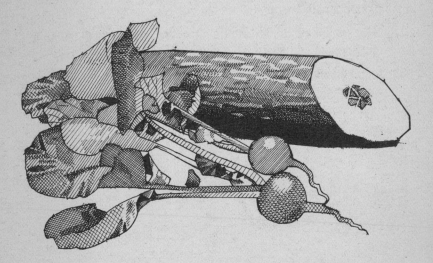

CHILLED AUBERGINES

Imperial (Metric)
1 lb (455g) small aubergines
1 tablespoonful soya sauce
1 tablespoonful sesame oil
1 tablespoonful raw cane sugar
1 teaspoonful sea salt
½ teaspoonful ground ginger

American
1 pound small eggplants
1 tablespoonful soy sauce
1 tablespoonful sesame oil
1 tablespoonful raw cane sugar
1 teaspoonful sea salt
½ teaspoonful ground ginger

1. Remove stems from aubergines (eggplants) and place immediately in pan of cold water (water must cover them or they will become discoloured), bring to boil and then allow to simmer for 15-20 minutes until tender.

2. Mix remaining ingredients together to make a dressing.

3. When aubergines (eggplants) are cooked, remove from heat, drain and cut into quarters lengthwise.

4. Pour dressing evenly over quartered aubergines (eggplants), chill and serve.

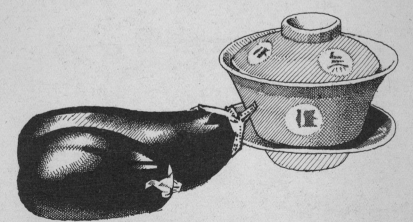

SPICED SOYA BEANS

Imperial (Metric)
1 lb (455g) unshelled soya beans
1 tablespoonful sea salt
1 red pepper, chopped
1 clove aniseed
½ teaspoonful freshly ground black
  pepper

American
1 pound unshelled soy beans
1 tablespoonful sea salt
1 red pepper, chopped
1 clove aniseed
½ teaspoonful freshly ground black
  pepper

1. Wash and cut ends off soya beans.

2. Place sufficient water in a pan to cover soya beans and bring to boil.

3. Add salt, chopped red pepper, aniseed and soya beans; boil for 15 minutes.

4. Remove from heat, drain and sprinkle with black pepper. Serve chilled (pods are discarded when eating).

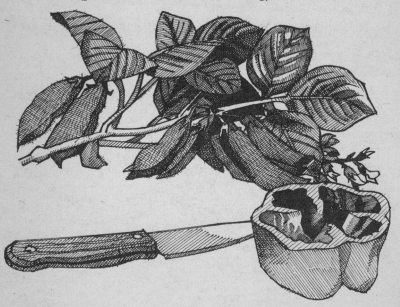

BROCCOLI SALAD WITH GOLDEN SAUCE

Imperial (Metric)	American
½ lb (225g) broccoli florets	8 ounces broccoli florets
¼ teaspoonful sea salt	¼ teaspoonful sea salt
3 egg yolks	3 egg yolks
2 tablespoonsful raw cane sugar	2 tablespoonsful raw cane sugar
3 tablespoonsful wine vinegar	3 tablespoonsful wine vinegar
1 tablespoonful cornflour	1 tablespoonful cornstarch
2 teaspoonsful horseradish	2 teaspoonsful horseradish
4 medium red radishes	4 medium red radishes

1. Bring a saucepan of salted water to the boil and drop in the broccoli florets. Cook for 1 minute, drain and chill.

2. Put the egg yolks, salt, sugar, vinegar and cornflour in a basin and beat until smooth. Pour into the top of a double boiler and cook over boiling water, stirring constantly, until the mixture thickens (about 5-6 minutes).

3. Stir in the horseradish, remove from heat and leave to cool.

4. Top and tail the washed radishes and then cut into paper-thin slices.

5. Place chilled broccoli on a serving plate, pour the cold sauce over it and decorate with the radish slices.

CUCUMBER AND SEAWEED SALAD

Imperial (Metric)	American
4 oz (115g) dried lobe-leaf seaweed (*wakami*)	4 ounces dried lobe-leaf seaweed (*wakami*)
1 cucumber	1 cucumber
Sea salt	Sea salt
4 tablespoonsful wine vinegar	4 tablespoonsful wine vinegar
3 tablespoonsful soya sauce	3 tablespoonsful soy sauce
2 teaspoonsful raw cane sugar	2 teaspoonsful raw cane sugar
¼ teaspoonful sea salt	¼ teaspoonful sea salt

1. Soak the seaweed in cold water for about 20-30 minutes until it softens. Drain and cut into 1½ in. (3.5cm) lengths.

2. Wash but do not peel the cucumber, cut into thin slices, discard the two end pieces, sprinkle the rest with salt and leave to stand for 30 minutes. Pat dry with a clean cloth or absorbent paper, put into a serving dish with the seaweed.

3. Mix the vinegar, soya sauce, sugar and salt together in a bowl or jug, pour over the cucumber and seaweed, tossing gently to mix thoroughly. Serve cold.

CHILLED LOTUS ROOT

Imperial (Metric)	American
¼ pint (140ml) cold water	⅔ cupful cold water
1 tablespoonful cider vinegar	1 tablespoonful cider vinegar
1 lotus root	1 lotus root
¼ pint (140ml) rice wine	⅔ cupful rice wine
4 tablespoonsful raw cane sugar	4 tablespoonsful raw cane sugar
½ teaspoonful sea salt	½ teaspoonful sea salt
Finely chopped red pepper to garnish	Finely chopped red pepper to garnish

1. Place the water and vinegar in a small saucepan, but do not yet heat.

2. Wash and peel the lotus root, cut into thin slices, horizontally, and put each slice into the saucepan immediately it is cut.

3. Bring the contents of the saucepan to the boil and cook for 2-3 minutes until the lotus root is tender but still crisp. Remove the lotus root from the pan and leave to drain.

4. Add all the other ingredients to the pan of vinegared water, bring to the boil, reduce heat and stir until all the sugar has dissolved.

5. Remove the pan from the heat, pour the liquid over the lotus root slices and leave to soak for 20 minutes.

6. Drain well and serve chilled. Garnish with finely chopped red pepper.

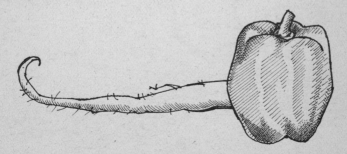

4.

EGG DISHES

EGG SALAD

Imperial (Metric)	American
6 hard-boiled eggs, shelled and halved	6 hard-boiled eggs, shelled and halved
1 tablespoonful vegetable oil	1 tablespoonful vegetable oil
1 teaspoonful chilli powder	1 teaspoonful chilli powder
½ teaspoonful cumin seeds, finely ground	½ teaspoonful cumin seeds, finely ground
½ teaspoonful cardamom seeds, finely ground	½ teaspoonful cardamom seeds, finely ground
½ lb (225g) curd cheese or plain yogurt	8 ounces curd cheese or plain yogurt
Grated rind and juice of 1 lime or lemon	Grated rind and juice of 1 lime or lemon
Chopped coriander leaves or parsley to garnish	Chopped cilantro or parsley to garnish

1. Place the egg halves neatly on a serving dish, cut side up.

2. Heat the oil in a pan and lightly fry the spices for 2-3 minutes to remove their raw flavour. Allow to cool.

3. Beat the curd cheese or yogurt until it is smooth, add the spices and lime juice and rind, blend well and then pour evenly over the egg halves.

4. Garnish with chopped coriander leaves (cilantro) and serve cold.

CHILLIED EGGS

Imperial (Metric)	American
2 tablespoonsful vegetable oil	2 tablespoonsful vegetable oil
1 onion, finely chopped	1 onion, finely chopped
4 dried red chillies, de-seeded and finely chopped	4 dried red chillies, de-seeded and finely chopped
¼ teaspoonful turmeric powder	¼ teaspoonful turmeric powder
1 teaspoonful ground ginger	1 teaspoonful ground ginger
¼ teaspoonful salt	¼ teaspoonful salt
8 eggs	8 eggs
2 spring onions, finely chopped, and soya sauce to garnish	2 scallions, finely chopped, and soy sauce to garnish

1. Heat the oil in a pan, add the chopped onion and chillies and fry lightly.

2. Beat the eggs well in a bowl, add the spices, mix well, then pour into the pan with the fried onions and chillies.

3. Stir well and cook until firm. Serve immediately, sprinkled with soya sauce and garnished with chopped spring onions (scallions).

STEAMED EGG CUSTARD

Imperial (Metric)	American
4 eggs	4 eggs
½ teaspoonful sea salt	½ teaspoonful sea salt
¼ teaspoonful freshly ground black pepper	¼ teaspoonful freshly ground black pepper
1 pint (570ml) hot vegetable stock or water	2½ cupsful hot vegetable stock or water
4 spring onions, finely chopped	4 scallions, finely chopped
2 tablespoonsful soya sauce	2 tablespoonsful soy sauce

1. Break the eggs into a mixing bowl, beat well, add the salt and pepper.

2. Stir in the hot stock or water, pour into a heated serving dish, sprinkle with chopped spring onions (scallions), place in a steamer and steam for 15-20 minutes.

3. Sprinkle with soya sauce immediately before serving.

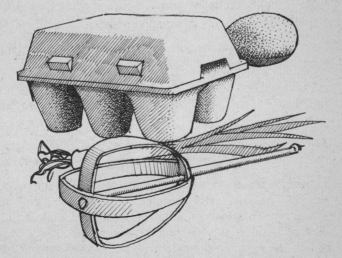

EGG AND MUSHROOM CURRY

Imperial (Metric)	American
Eggs (allow 1 egg per person)	Eggs (allow 1 egg per person)
1 small red onion	1 small red onion
1 clove garlic	1 clove garlic
1 medium tomato	1 medium tomato
Small piece of fresh ginger	Small piece of fresh ginger
2 tablespoonsful ghee or coconut oil	2 tablespoonsful ghee or coconut oil
Few curry leaves	Few curry leaves
1 teaspoonful garam masala	1 teaspoonful garam masala
½ teaspoonful chilli powder	½ teaspoonful chilli powder
¼ teaspoonful turmeric powder	¼ teaspoonful turmeric powder
¼ teaspoonful sea salt	¼ teaspoonful sea salt
½ pint (285ml) thick santan (page 109)	1⅓ cupsful thick santan (page 109)
4 large dried mushrooms, soaked	4 large dried mushrooms, soaked
Juice of 1 lime or lemon	Juice of 1 lime or lemon

1. Hard-boil the eggs, cool and remove their shells; cut each egg into two lengthwise.

2. Skin the onion, garlic, tomato and ginger; slice them all thinly.

3. Heat the ghee or oil in a pan and lightly fry the onion, garlic and ginger.

4. Add the washed curry leaves, garam masala, chilli and turmeric powder. Fry, stirring gently, until the spices separate from the ghee or oil.

5. Add the salt and santan, bring to simmering point, stirring all the time, until the sauce thickens.

6. Drain the soaked mushrooms, slice and add to the mixture in the pan. Simmer for 5 minutes then add the sliced tomato; continue cooking for 2-3 minutes until the tomato is soft. Carefully add the halved eggs to the mixture, cover the pan for 2-3 minutes to heat the eggs, remove carefully to a warmed serving dish and pour the sauce over them.

7. Sprinkle with lime juice and serve immediately.

SPICED EGGS

Imperial (Metric)
8 eggs
1 oz (30g) black tea leaves
1 stick cinnamon
2 pieces star anise
2 tablespoonsful soya sauce
2 teaspoonsful sea salt
2 teaspoonsful raw cane sugar
Chopped parsley to garnish (optional)

American
8 eggs
1 ounce black tea leaves
1 stick cinnamon
2 pieces star anise
2 tablespoonsful soy sauce
2 teaspoonsful sea salt
2 teaspoonsful raw cane sugar
Chopped parsley to garnish (optional)

1. Place the eggs in a saucepan, cover with cold water and bring slowly to the boil so that the shells do not crack. When water boils, reduce heat and simmer for 15 minutes, leave to cool then drain.

2. Using the back of a heavy spoon, crack the egg shells all over but do not peel.

3. Place the cracked eggs in a large saucepan, add sufficient water to cover them, then add all the other ingredients. Bring to the boil.

4. Partially cover the pan, simmer the eggs for 2-3 hours, drain and cool.

5. Just before serving, carefully remove the shells and cut the eggs into quarters lengthwise. Sprinkle with chopped parsley if desired.

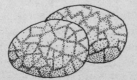

SPINACH ROLLS

Imperial (Metric)
½ lb (225g) fresh spinach
4 eggs
½ teaspoonful sea salt
2 tablespoonsful vegetable oil
Soya sauce for garnish

American
8 ounces fresh spinach
4 eggs
½ teaspoonful sea salt
2 tablespoonsful vegetable oil
Soy sauce for garnish

1. Wash spinach, then boil in a little salted water for 3-4 minutes in a covered pan.

2. Drain off the water and squeeze the spinach until all excess water has gone.

3. Break the eggs into a basin and beat well with the salt.

4. Heat a little oil in a pan and, when it is moderately hot, pour a quarter of the beaten egg into the pan, tilting it gently so that the bottom of the pan is completely covered. Cook gently until omelette is just firm. Remove carefully and reserve on a covered, heated plate.

5. Repeat this process until all the egg mixture has been used up. It should make 4 omelettes.

6. Place a quarter of the cooked spinach down the centre of each omelette, then roll each omelette over to form a firm cylinder.

7. Cut each omelette in half, diagonally, sprinkle with soya sauce and serve.

BRAISED EGGS

Imperial (Metric)	American
4 eggs	4 eggs
1 bamboo shoot, sliced	1 bamboo shoot, sliced
2 mushrooms, sliced	2 mushrooms, sliced
4 tablespoons soya sauce	4 tablespoons soy sauce
1 teaspoonful raw cane sugar	1 teaspoonful raw cane sugar
1 teaspoonful cornflour	1 teaspoonful cornstarch
1 tablespoonful wine	1 tablespoonful wine
4 oz (115g) wholemeal flour	1 cupful wholewheat flour
Vegetable oil for deep-frying	Vegetable oil for deep-frying

1. Boil the eggs for 5 minutes, then carefully remove their shells and leave to cool.

2. Boil the sliced bamboo shoot and mushrooms for 5 minutes, drain and set aside.

3. Mix the soya sauce, sugar, cornflour and wine together in a small basin and soak the eggs in this sauce for 3-4 minutes before rolling them in the flour.

4. Pour sufficient oil into a pan for deep-frying. Heat the oil and fry the coated eggs until they are brown; remove the eggs and drain the pan.

5. Reheat the pan and add 3 tablespoonsful of the oil. Put the bamboo shoots, mushrooms and sauce mixture in the pan and stir gently to blend.

6. Add the eggs, simmer for about 1 minute and serve immediately on a bed of rice or noodles.

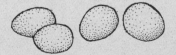

CHINESE OMELETTE

Imperial (Metric)	American
Vegetable oil for frying	Vegetable oil for frying
6 spring onions, chopped	6 scallions, chopped
1 stick of celery, thinly sliced	1 stalk of celery, thinly sliced
½ lb (225g) bean sprouts	8 ounces bean sprouts
4 dried mushrooms, soaked and sliced	4 dried mushrooms, soaked and sliced
1 slice fresh ginger, minced	1 slice fresh ginger, minced
1 teaspoonful sea salt	1 teaspoonful sea salt
½ teaspoonful freshly ground black pepper	½ teaspoonful freshly ground black pepper
4 eggs	4 eggs
Soya sauce and chopped parsley for garnish	Soy sauce and chopped parsley for garnish

1. Heat a little oil in a pan and fry the spring onions (scallions), celery, bean sprouts, mushrooms, ginger, salt and pepper until all ingredients are cooked.

2. In a separate basin, beat the eggs lightly, add salt and pepper to taste, then add the cooked ingredients and mix well.

3. Heat more oil in the pan (about 1 tablespoonful), pour in just sufficient omelette mixture to form a small omelette, fry on both sides until golden brown, remove to heated serving dish and cover.

4. Repeat this process until all the omelette mixture has been used up.

5. Sprinkle the cooked omelettes with soya sauce, garnish with chopped parsley and serve hot or cold.

5.

SIDE DISHES

FRIED RICE BALLS

Imperial (Metric)
2 tomatoes, blanched and skinned
2 small red onions, chopped
Vegetable oil for deep-frying
¾ lb (340g) boiled brown rice, at
   least 1 day old
2 eggs, lightly beaten
1 egg mixed with wholemeal
   breadcrumbs for coating
Chilli Sauce (page 116)

American
2 tomatoes, blanched and skinned
2 small red onions, chopped
Vegetable oil for deep-frying
12 ounces boiled brown rice, at least
   1 day old
2 eggs, lightly beaten
1 egg mixed with wholewheat
   breadcrumbs for coating
Chilli Sauce (page 116)

1. Lightly fry the tomatoes and chopped onions together in a little oil.

2. Add the boiled rice and sufficient beaten egg to bind the mixture together. Stir with a wooden spoon over a very low heat until all the ingredients are completely blended. Turn on to a plate, cover and leave to cool.

3. Break off pieces of the cooled mixture and roll them into balls about the size of walnuts. Coat each ball in egg and breadcrumbs until all the ingredients have been used up.

4. Heat oil in a pan and deep-fry the rice balls until they are golden brown. Drain onto absorbent paper and serve immediately with Chilli Sauce.

ONION BHAJJIAS

Imperial (Metric)	American
4 tablespoonsful gram flour	4 tablespoonsful gram flour
1 egg	1 egg
1 teaspoonful ground coriander	1 teaspoonful ground coriander
1 teaspoonful ground cumin	1 teaspoonful ground cumin
1 teaspoonful ground turmeric	1 teaspoonful ground turmeric
½ teaspoonful chilli powder	½ teaspoonful chilli powder
½ teaspoonful ground aniseed	½ teaspoonful ground aniseed
2 large onions, peeled and finely sliced	2 large onions, peeled and finely sliced
Vegetable oil for deep-frying	Vegetable oil for deep-frying

1. Make a thick batter with the flour and egg. Mix in a little cold water a teaspoonful at a time until the batter will drop easily from a spoon.

2. Add the ground spices and the sliced onion, mix thoroughly.

3. Heat oil in a pan until it reaches haze heat, drop in the batter mixture a tablespoonful at a time and deep-fry until golden brown.

4. Drain and serve with a spicy sauce in a separate dish.

Note: Any left-over cooked vegetables can be used to supplement or replace the onions in this recipe.

STEAMED AUBERGINE WITH EGG

Imperial (Metric)	American
2 lb (900g) small aubergines	2 pounds small eggplants
1 large leek	1 large leek
2 eggs	2 eggs
3 tablespoonsful soya sauce	3 tablespoonsful soy sauce
1 tablespoonful raw cane sugar	1 tablespoonful raw cane sugar
4 tablespoonsful vegetable oil	4 tablespoonsful vegetable oil

1. Wash the aubergines (eggplants) and remove stems. Steam for 15-20 minutes until tender.

2. Wash leek and chop into small pieces.

3. Beat eggs in a bowl, add chopped leek, soya sauce and sugar; mix well.

4. Heat oil and sauté the egg mixture. When set, break up into small pieces with a fork.

5. Cut aubergines (eggplants) into quarters lengthwise and arrange in circle around serving plate or dish.

6. Place egg mixture in the centre and serve hot.

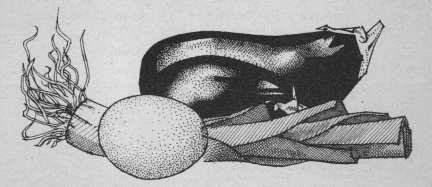

FRIED CURRY PUFFS

Imperial (Metric)	American
1 tin mixed vegetables to yield 10 oz (285g) drained weight	1 can mixed vegetables to yield 10 ounces drained weight
¼ teaspoonful turmeric	¼ teaspoonful turmeric
¼ teaspoonful chilli powder	¼ teaspoonful chilli powder
¼ teaspoonful cumin	¼ teaspoonful cumin
Pinch of sea salt	Pinch of sea salt
½ lb (225g) wholemeal flour	2 cupsful wholewheat flour
2 oz (55g) polyunsaturated margarine	¼ cupful polyunsaturated margarine
¼ teaspoonful baking powder	¼ teaspoonful baking soda
1 egg, lightly beaten	1 egg, lightly beaten
Vegetable oil for cooking	Vegetable oil for cooking

1. Place drained vegetables in a bowl, add spices and salt, mix well with a fork.

2. Sift flour and baking powder into a bowl, add margarine and work it lightly into the flour using your fingers.

3. When mixture has texture of fine breadcrumbs, add beaten egg and form into a soft dough, adding a few drops of cold water if necessary.

4. Continue to knead dough for about 5 minutes then roll the dough out on a floured board until it is about ⅛ in. (2mm) thick. Cut into rounds about 4 in. (10cm) in diameter until all the dough is used up.

5. Place a heap of curried vegetable mixture in the centre of each round, fold the dough over and press the edges together firmly; flute the edges.

6. Fry the curry puffs in hot oil until golden brown on both sides and drain on kitchen paper before serving.

BEAN SPROUTS WITH GREEN PEPPERS

Imperial (Metric)	American
1 lb (455g) bean sprouts	1 pound bean sprouts
3 green peppers	3 green peppers
5 tablespoonful vegetable oil	5 tablespoonful vegetable oil
2 tablespoonful white wine	2 tablespoonful white wine
1 teaspoonful sea salt	1 teaspoonful sea salt

1. Remove heads and tails from bean sprouts and leave prepared sprouts in water until ready to use.

2. Wash, seed and shred green peppers.

3. Heat oil and fry drained bean sprouts and shredded peppers until latter are tender but still crisp.

4. Add wine and salt just before serving.

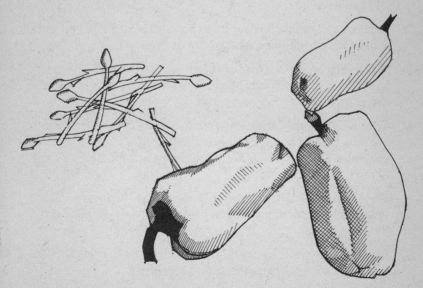

FRIED BUTTER BEANS

Imperial (Metric)	American
5 tablespoonsful vegetable oil	5 tablespoonsful vegetable oil
1 lb (455g) shelled butter beans	1 pound shelled Lima beans
¼ pint (140ml) water	⅔ cupful water
3 tablespoonsful raw cane sugar	3 tablespoonsful raw cane sugar
1 tablespoonful sea salt	1 tablespoonful sea salt

1. Heat oil and fry beans gently until their colour intensifies.

2. Add water and seasoning; boil over high flame for further 5 minutes.

3. Serve hot or cold.

Note: If the beans are bought unshelled, you will need approximately 4 pounds (1.8 kilos) to obtain 1 pound (455g) shelled beans.

VEGETABLE ROLLS

Imperial (Metric)	American
8 bean curd 'paper' sheets	8 bean curd 'paper' sheets
½ lb (225g) yellow bean curd	8 ounces yellow bean curd
4 oz (115g) chopped spinach (or other greens)	4 ounces chopped spinach (or other greens)
4 large dried mushrooms, soaked	4 large dried mushrooms, soaked
½ lb (225g) tin bamboo shoots, drained	8 ounce can bamboo shoots, drained
½ teaspoonful sea salt	½ teaspoonful sea salt
½ teaspoonful white wine	½ teaspoonful white wine
½ teaspoonful sesame oil	½ teaspoonful sesame oil
3 tablespoonsful vegetable oil	3 tablespoonsful vegetable oil
4 tablespoonsful vegetable stock	4 tablespoonsful vegetable stock
2 teaspoonsful soya sauce	2 teaspoonsful soy sauce

1. Soak bean curd sheets for about 1 minute until soft enough to fold.

2. Mash bean curd and mix with spinach, chopped mushrooms, drained and chopped bamboo shoots, salt, wine and sesame oil.

3. Lay bean curd sheets flat and place 1½ tablespoonsful of mixture in middle of each sheet.

4. Form rolls by folding bottom edge of sheets up, left and right edges over, then rolling towards the top carefully.

5. Heat oil (very hot) and fry rolls on both sides till crisp and golden.

6. Lower heat, add stock and soya sauce, simmer for about 10 minutes until all liquid is absorbed. Serve hot.

BRAISED BEAN CURD

Imperial (Metric)	American
1½ lb (680g) bean curd	3 cupsful bean curd
2 oz (55g) wholemeal flour	½ cupful wholewheat flour
2 eggs	2 eggs
½ teaspoonful sea salt	½ teaspoonful sea salt
¼ pint (140ml) vegetable oil	⅔ cupful vegetable oil
4 dried mushrooms, soaked	4 dried mushrooms, soaked
1 large leek, chopped	1 large leek, chopped
¾ pint (425ml) vegetable stock	2 cupsful vegetable stock
2 teaspoonsful soya sauce	2 teaspoonsful soy sauce
1 teaspoonful sea salt	1 teaspoonful sea salt
2 tablespoonsful wine	2 tablespoonsful wine
1½ teaspoonsful cornflour	1½ teaspoonsful cornstarch
3 tablespoonsful water	3 tablespoonsful water

1. Press bean curd cake gently between two plates in order to squeeze out any liquid, drain off.

2. Cut bean curd into thick slices about 4 in. × 4 in. × ½ in. (10cm × 10cm × 1.5cm).

3. Mix flour, eggs and ½ teaspoonful of salt together to form batter.

4. Heat 6 tablespoonsful of the oil. Coat bean curd squares with batter and fry on both sides until golden brown; remove to warm place.

5. Add remaining oil to pan and fry sliced mushroom and chopped leek.

6. Add bean curd, stock, seasonings and cornflour mixed to smooth paste with water. Serve hot.

POTATO FRITTERS

Imperial (Metric)
1½ lb (680g) potatoes
4 large dried mushrooms
2 tablespoonsful soya sauce
½ tablespoonful sea salt
2 oz (55g) wholemeal flour
6 tablespoonsful vegetable oil
1 small bamboo shoot, sliced
2 oz (55g) green peas or soya beans
½ pint (285ml) water with
  ½ teaspoonful sea salt

American
1½ pounds potatoes
4 large dried mushrooms
2 tablespoonsful soy sauce
½ tablespoonful sea salt
½ cupful wholewheat flour
6 tablespoonsful vegetable oil
1 small bamboo shoot, sliced
⅓ cupful green peas or soy beans
1⅓ cupsful water with
  ½ teaspoonful sea salt

1. Peel and boil potatoes.

2. Soak mushrooms in lukewarm water for at least 10 minutes; drain but save juice.

3. Drain and mash potatoes adding soya sauce, 3 tablespoonsful of juice from mushrooms and salt.

4. Heat over a low flame adding flour. Continue to cook gently until mixture thickens, stirring all the time.

5. Remove from heat, divide into quarters and shape into circular 'cakes'.

6. Heat 4 tablespoonsful oil, fry potato cakes on both sides to a light golden brown; remove to a plate.

7. Heat remaining 2 tablespoonsful oil and sauté the vegetables. Add salted water.

8. Add potato fritters and boil for about 15 minutes or until liquid has evaporated. Serve hot.

6.

RICE AND NOODLES

Rice and noodles are the staple foods of the Orient and virtually every meal served in the Far East will be accompanied by one or more dishes prepared from these basic ingredients. So, here are some main dishes using rice or noodles, starting with simple instructions on their preparation.

General advice
Long-grain rice is the best type for making plain boiled rice or rice dishes although the shorter variety can be used. However, short-grain rice needs slightly less water than the long-grain and, as all the recipes in this book are for long-grain rice, adjustments must be made if you use the shorter type.

When cooking boiled rice, never stir the rice and try to refrain from lifting the lid during the first 20 minutes to see how it is getting along. As cooking times vary considerably acording to the amount of rice used, you will have to look after 20 minutes; when natural steam holes are formed in the dull dry surface of the rice it is ready and each grain should be separate when it is served.

Uncooked rice doubles in volume when boiled. It keeps well in a refrigerator for 5 or 6 days and can be used for fried rice. Indeed, freshly boiled rice is never used for frying; the rice should be at least 1 day old, and preferably 2 or 3.

PLAIN BOILED BROWN RICE
Serves 1

Imperial (Metric)
6 oz (170g) uncooked brown rice
½ pint (285ml) water

American
¾ cupful uncooked brown rice
1⅓ cupsful water

1. Wash the rice thoroughly in cold water by agitating it with your hand. Drain away the water and repeat the process several times until the water appears completely clear.

2. Put rice and water (in proportions above) in large pan.

3. Bring quickly to the boil over a high flame and then reduce the heat as low as it will go and cover pan with lid.

4. Continue to cook very slowly, without stirring, until all the water has been absorbed and the rice has a good, flaky texture.

Note: This method achieves excellent results although a hard crust of rice may remain at the bottom of the pan; this is removed easily if left to soak.

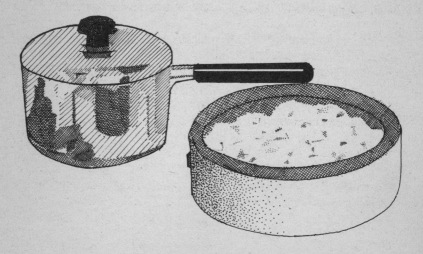

FRIED RICE

Imperial (Metric)	American
2 tablespoonsful vegetable oil	2 tablespoonsful vegetable oil
3 cupsful boiled brown rice at least 1 day old	4 cupsful boiled brown rice at least 1 day old
1 teaspoonful sea salt	1 teaspoonful sea salt
½ teaspoonful freshly ground pepper	½ teaspoonful freshly ground pepper
3 eggs	3 eggs
4 spring onions, chopped fine	4 scallions, chopped fine
Small bunch parsley leaves, coarsely chopped	Small bunch parsley leaves, coarsely chopped
2 tablespoonsful soya sauce	2 tablespoonsful soy sauce

1. Heat oil in pan and toss in rice. Fry until rice is hot, stirring gently, and pressing out any lumps that have formed, with a wooden spoon.

2. Add salt and pepper; mix in with rice.

3. Make a well in the centre of the rice with a spoon or fork and break the eggs into this hollow, stirring them with a fork.

4. When eggs are semi-cooked, stir thoroughly into the rice. Add parsley.

5. Remove from heat, place on heated serving dish and sprinkle with soya sauce.

YELLOW RICE

Imperial (Metric)
2 tablespoonsful ghee
Small piece fresh ginger, chopped finely
3 small red onions, finely sliced
2 cloves garlic, crushed
½ teaspoonful saffron
3 cupsful uncooked brown rice
¼ teaspoonful cardamom seeds
1 in. (2.5cm) cinnamon stick
4 cloves
2 in. (5cm) piece lemon grass
2 bay leaves
¼ teaspoonful sea salt
½ pint (285ml) thick santan (page 109)
¼ pint (140ml) water

American
2 tablespoonsful ghee
Small piece fresh ginger, chopped finely
3 small red onions, finely sliced
2 cloves garlic, crushed
½ teaspoonful saffron
4 cupsful uncooked brown rice
¼ teaspoonful cardamom seeds
1 inch cinnamon stick
4 cloves
2 inch piece lemon grass
2 bay leaves
¼ teaspoonful sea salt
1⅓ cupsful thick santan (page 109)
⅔ cupful water

1. Melt the ghee in a pan and lightly fry together the ginger, onions, garlic and saffron.

2. Add the rice, cardamom seeds, cinnamon stick, cloves and lemon grass; continue to cook over a low flame, stirring occasionally, until all the ghee has been absorbed.

3. Add the remaining ingredients.

4. Cover the pan and simmer gently over a very low flame until the rice is completely cooked.

5. Remove from direct heat and leave to dry out completely by the side of the stove or similar warm place (about 3-4 minutes). Remove lemon grass, bay leaves and cinnamon stick before serving. Serve with curry, vegetable dishes, sauces etc.

INDONESIAN FRIED RICE
Nasi Goreng

Imperial (Metric)	American
1 egg	1 egg
1 teaspoonful chopped parsley	1 teaspoonful chopped parsley
2 tablespoonsful vegetable oil	2 tablespoonsful vegetable oil
2 cloves garlic, chopped	2 cloves garlic, chopped
2 medium onions, peeled and sliced	2 medium onions, peeled and sliced
3 cupsful boiled brown rice	4 cupsful boiled brown rice
2 tablespoonsful sultanas	2 tablespoonsful golden seedless
2 tablespoonsful soya sauce	raisins
2 tablespoonsful tomato ketchup	2 tablespoonsful soy sauce
Few leaves watercress	2 tablespoonsful tomato catsup
2 spring onions, finely chopped	Few leaves watercress
	2 scallions, finely chopped

1. Beat the egg well and mix in the chopped parsley.

2. Heat a little of the oil and fry the egg on both sides; remove from pan, cut into thin slices and set aside on covered plate.

3. Add remainder of oil to pan and heat. Fry the garlic and onions until golden brown.

4. Stir in the boiled rice, sultanas (golden seedless raisins) and soya sauce; fry together over moderate flame until mixture is heated through and evenly coloured by the soya sauce.

5. Reduce heat and stir in the tomato ketchup.

6. Place on warm serving plate and garnish with egg strips, watercress and spring onions (scallions).

GLUTINOUS RICE CONGEE

Imperial (Metric)	American
½ lb (225g) uncooked glutinous brown rice	1 cupful uncooked glutinous brown rice
2 pints (1.14 litres) boiling water	5 cupsful boiling water
1 teaspoonful sea salt	1 teaspoonful sea salt
Small piece of fresh ginger, shredded	Small piece of fresh ginger, shredded
4 large dried mushrooms, soaked and sliced	4 large dried mushrooms, soaked and sliced
1 tablespoonful raw cane sugar	1 tablespoonful raw cane sugar
¼ teaspoonful freshly ground black pepper	¼ teaspoonful freshly ground black pepper
1 tablespoonful vegetable oil	1 tablespoonful vegetable oil
1 leek, chopped	1 leek, chopped
1 oz (30g) cashews or peanuts	¼ cupful cashews or peanuts
Parsley to garnish	Parsley to garnish

1. Wash rice thoroughly and put into large pan. Pour on the boiling water and salt. Cover with lid and simmer for about 45 minutes until rice is soft.

2. Add the ginger and mushrooms. Mix sugar, pepper and oil in small basin, then add to rice.

3. Simmer for 20 minutes. Add leeks and nuts and continue to cook for further 5 minutes to ensure that all ingredients are heated through.

4. Serve in individual heated rice bowls and garnish with chopped parsley.

SPICY RICE FRITTERS

Imperial (Metric)	American
1 green chilli	1 green chilli
1 red chilli	1 red chilli
½ teaspoonful turmeric powder	½ teaspoonful turmeric powder
Sea salt to taste	Sea salt to taste
4 small red onions	4 small red onions
Vegetable oil for frying	Vegetable oil for frying
1 lb (455g) ground rice	1 pound ground rice

1. Pound the chillies, turmeric and salt together.

2. Peel and chop the onions and fry lightly in a little oil. Add spices.

3. Mix the spices with the ground rice to form flat cakes, using a little oil to bind if necessary.

4. Shallow-fry the rice cakes in very hot oil until light golden brown on both sides. Serve with salad, vegetables or a well-flavoured sauce.

Noodles
Ready-made noodles, fresh or dried, can be obtained in most grocery
shops nowadays, yet they are so simple to make that I have included
the basic recipe here. There are two types of noodles, egg or plain,
but the method of making is the same.

PLAIN OR EGG NOODLES

Imperial (Metric)
1 lb (455g) plain wholemeal flour
¾ pint (425ml) water *or* 4 eggs
Cornflour

American
4 cupsful plain wholewheat flour
2 cupsful water *or* 4 eggs
Cornflour

1. Mix flour and eggs (or water) to a soft dough. Knead gently for
    about 5 minutes.

2. Dust a pastry board lightly with cornflour and roll out the dough
    on this as thinly as possible.

3. Dust the rolled dough lightly with cornflour then roll it round
    the rolling-pin and press with the palms of your hand.

4. Roll the dough out again and repeat the process four times.

5. Pleat the rolled dough (fold to the back and then to the front)
    neatly into approximately 4 in. (10cm) pleats. Do not remove
    any surplus dough at edge.

6. Cut the folded dough across the folds as thinly as possible with
    a sharp knife. The untidy 'end' of dough can be used for picking
    up the dough and shaking out the noodles which should separate
    easily due to dusting the layers with cornflour.

PREPARING NOODLES

Allow 6 ounces (170g) uncooked noodles per person

1. Prepare a large pan of fast-boiling water. Drop the noodles into the water and boil for about 3 minutes.

2. Turn out into colander, rinse in cold water, then drain. When thoroughly drained, the noodles can be used for soups or frying.

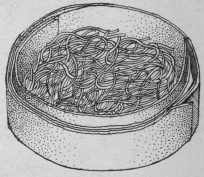

PLAIN FRIED NOODLES

Imperial (Metric)	American
1½ lb (680g) noodles (page 86)	1½ pounds noodles (page 86)
7 tablespoonsful vegetable oil	7 tablespoonsful vegetable oil
2 teaspoonsful sea salt	2 teaspoonsful sea salt
1½ tablespoonsful white wine	1½ tablespoonsful white wine
2 tablespoonsful soya sauce	2 tablespoonsful soy sauce

1. Boil noodles in salted water for 7 minutes, drain, rinse under running cold water and drain again.

2. Heat oil in a pan. Add drained noodles and, after 1 minute, the salt, wine and soya sauce.

3. Stir continuously but gently in order not to break the noodles. Continue to cook over a low heat for 5 minutes. Serve hot.

FRIED EGG NOODLES WITH VEGETABLES

Imperial (Metric)

6 oz (170g) egg noodles
(page 86)
2 tablespoonsful vegetable oil
2 cloves garlic
1 teaspoonful taucheo, finely ground
Sea salt and freshly ground black
pepper to taste
¾ pint (425ml) vegetable stock or
water
1 lb (455g) cabbage, shredded
½ lb (225g) carrots, shredded
½ lb (225g) French beans, shredded
1 lb (455g) bean sprouts
1-egg omelette and a few coriander
leaves or watercress to garnish

American

6 ounces egg noodles
(page 86)
2 tablespoonsful vegetable oil
2 cloves garlic
1 teaspoonful taucheo, finely ground
Sea salt and freshly ground black
pepper to taste
2 cupsful vegetable stock or water
1 pound shredded cabbage
1¼ cupsful shredded carrots
1¼ cupsful shredded French beans
1 pound bean sprouts
1-egg omelette and a few cilantro
leaves or watercress to garnish

1. Place noodles in deep pan, cover with boiling water, stir well then leave to soak for about 10 minutes until noodles are soft.

2. When ready, drain noodles, refill pan with cold water then transfer noodles to a colander and leave until water has completely drained away.

3. Heat oil, add crushed garlic and cook until golden brown.

4. Add taucheo, salt and pepper; continue cooking over low heat for 5 minutes.

5. Add stock, bring to the boil and add shredded vegetables; cover pan and simmer for 5-10 minutes.

6. Remove lid, add noodles and bean sprouts; mix together thoroughly but gently.

7. Remove to heated serving dish and garnish with the omelette, cut into fine strips, and chopped coriander leaves (cilantro) or watercress. Serve with well-flavoured sauce, Chinese gravy or sambal.

CHILLED NOODLES WITH SPICY SAUCE

Imperial (Metric)

¾ lb (340g) egg noodles (page 86)
2 tablespoonsful sesame oil
1 egg
6 in. (15cm) length cucumber, peeled and shredded
2 tablespoonsful sesame seeds, dry roasted
3 cloves garlic
2 tablespoonsful sesame oil
1 tablespoonful *Tabasco*
1 tablespoonful wine vinegar
2 tablespoonsful soya sauce
2 teaspoonsful raw cane sugar
¼ teaspoonful sea salt
½ pint (285ml) vegetable stock or water

American

12 ounces egg noodles (page 86)
2 tablespoonsful sesame oil
1 egg
6 in. length cucumber, peeled and shredded
2 tablespoonsful sesame seeds, dry roasted
3 cloves garlic
2 tablespoonsful sesame oil
1 tablespoonful *Tabasco*
1 tablespoonful wine vinegar
2 tablespoonsful soy sauce
2 teaspoonsful raw cane sugar
¼ teaspoonful sea salt
1⅓ cupsful vegetable stock or water

1. Drop noodles into pan of boiling salted water, cook for 5 minutes, drain, rinse under running cold water, drain.

2. Place in serving dish, add 2 tablespoonsful sesame oil, toss well, leave to cool.

3. Lightly beat the egg, fry in a little oil, drain and cut into thin strips.

4. Place the shredded egg and cucumber on top of the noodles and put in the fridge to chill.

5. Grind the sesame seeds and garlic together in a mortar.

6. Put the sesame oil, *Tabasco*, vinegar, soya sauce, sugar and salt into a mixing bowl, blend together and then add the ground sesame seeds and garlic. Add the water or stock and stir vigorously.

7. Either serve the sauce and chilled noodles in separate bowls or pour the sauce over the garnished noodles immediately before serving.

CRISPY NOODLES WITH EGGS

Imperial (Metric)
1 lb (450g) rice noodles
Vegetable oil for frying
2 small red onions, finely chopped
4 cloves garlic, chopped
½ lb (225g) yellow bean curd,
    shredded
2 tablespoonsful raw cane sugar
6 tablespoonsful wine vinegar
4 tablespoonsful soya sauce
4 oz (115g) fresh bean sprouts
4 eggs, lightly beaten
Finely chopped spring onions, red
    chillies and coriander leaves to
    garnish

American
1 pound rice noodles
Vegetable oil for frying
2 small red onions, finely chopped
4 cloves garlic, chopped
8 ounces yellow bean curd,
    shredded
2 tablespoonsful raw cane sugar
6 tablespoonsful wine vinegar
4 tablespoonsful soy sauce
4 ounces fresh bean sprouts
4 eggs, lightly beaten
Finely chopped scallions, red chillies
    and cilantro to garnish

1. Scald the noodles in fast-boiling water, drain and leave in a warm place to dry thoroughly for about 30 minutes.

2. Heat oil in pan and deep-fry the noodles until crisp and light brown; remove carefully from the pan and set aside to drain on absorbent paper.

3. Pour out most of the oil from the pan, leaving about 1 tablespoonful, and fry the onions and garlic for 2-3 minutes.

4. Add the shredded bean curd and, when this is golden brown, add the sugar, vinegar and soya sauce, stirring well.

5. Stir in the washed bean sprouts, then gradually pour the beaten eggs into the pan, stirring well with a wooden spoon or spatula. Continue to cook for 2-3 minutes until the egg is soft-set.

6. Either place all the ingredients from the pan on a warm serving plate and top with the crispy noodles or add the noodles to the ingredients in the pan and mix thoroughly before turning out on to a serving dish.

7. Garnish and serve hot.

7.
DESSERTS

ROSEWATER PUDDING

Imperial (Metric)	American
¼ teaspoonful saffron	¼ teaspoonful saffron
1 teaspoonful rosewater	1 teaspoonful rosewater
1 lb (455g) curd or cream cheese	2 cupsful curd or cream cheese
6 oz (170g) raw cane sugar, powdered in a grinder	1 cupful raw cane sugar, powdered in a grinder
¼ teaspoonful ground cloves	¼ teaspoonful ground cloves
¼ teaspoonful ground cinnamon	¼ teaspoonful ground cinnamon
¼ teaspoonful ground nutmeg	¼ teaspoonful ground nutmeg
A few finely chopped nuts to garnish	A few finely chopped nuts to garnish

1. Soak the saffron in the rosewater until it has dissolved.

2. Blend the saffron and rosewater into the curd cheese, add all the other ingredients and beat vigorously until thoroughly blended and creamy smooth (this can be done using an electric blender).

3. Serve chilled, garnished with chopped nuts.

CANDIED APPLE SLICES

Imperial (Metric)	American
2 or 3 firm apples (about 1 lb/455g)	2 or 3 firm apples (about 1 pound)
Lemon juice	Lemon juice
2 egg whites	2 egg whites
2 tablespoonsful cornflour	2 tablespoonsful cornstarch
2 tablespoonsful plain wholemeal flour	2 tablespoonsful plain wholewheat flour
Vegetable oil for deep-frying	Vegetable oil for deep-frying
3 fl oz (90ml) water	1/3 cupful water
1/2 lb (225g) raw cane sugar	1 1/3 cupsful raw cane sugar
1/2 teaspoonful wine vinegar	1/2 teaspoonful wine vinegar
1 tablespoonful sesame seeds, dry roasted	1 tablespoonful sesame seeds, dry roasted
Bowl of ice-cold water	Bowl of ice-cold water

1. Peel and core the apples, then cut into 12 slices. Sprinkle thoroughly with lemon juice to prevent discolouration and set aside on a plate.

2. Mix the egg whites, cornflour and flour together to form a batter. Put the apple slices into the batter and turn each frequently in order to ensure that they are well coated with batter mixture.

3. Heat oil in a pan and when it is haze hot add the coated apple slices. Cook until golden brown, about 10 minutes, then drain.

4. Prepare a serving dish or plate large enough to accommodate the apple slices by oiling or greasing it thoroughly (this is essential).

5. In a large saucepan or wok pour the water and sugar. Cook, stirring continuously, until the sugar forms threads. Test the syrup by dropping a few drops into cold water and, when it reaches the hard-crack stage, it is ready.

6. Add the vinegar and sesame seeds to the syrup, stir well to mix, then add the apple slices and coat these thoroughly with the hot syrup.

7. Remove the apple slices on to the prepared serving dish or plate and serve immediately with a separate bowl of ice-cold water. Each apple slice is dipped in the cold water before eating.

Note: Bananas may be substituted for apples.

JAVA BANANA MOULD

Imperial (Metric)
2 large, ripe bananas
4 oz (115g) green pea flour
1 pint (570ml) thick santan
  (page 109)
6 tablespoonsful raw cane sugar
Few drops natural green food
  colouring

American
2 large, ripe bananas
1 cupful green pea flour
2½ cupsful thick santan (page 109)
6 tablespoonsful raw cane sugar
Few drops natural green food
  colouring

1. Steam the washed bananas for about 10 minutes until their skins are soft.

2. Blend the flour to a smooth paste with a little of the thick santan. Pour the rest of the santan into a saucepan, add the blended flour and bring slowly to the boil, stirring continuously, until the mixture is thick enough to coat the back of the spoon, then reduce the heat.

3. Simmer for 2-3 minutes more, then stir in the sugar until it has dissolved.

4. Peel the bananas and cut into thin slices.

5. Pour half the hot mixture into a wetted jelly mould or individual dishes and distribute the banana slices on the top. Quickly colour the remaining mixture then pour this over the banana layer.

6. Cover the mould with a plate and stand it in a basin of cold water to cool.

7. When the jelly is firm enough to leave the sides of the mould, carefully turn it out on to a plate, cut into neat pieces and serve chilled.

SWEET PORRIDGE

Imperial (Metric)
1 heaped tablespoonful seedless
   raisins or sultanas
2 tablespoonsful pea flour
2 tablespoonsful brown rice flour
¾ pint (425ml) thick santan
   (page 109)
½ teaspoonful pure vanilla essence
4 tablespoonsful raw cane sugar
¼ pint (140ml) thin santan
   (page 109)
A few chopped nuts to garnish

American
1 heaped tablespoonful seedless
   raisins or golden seedless raisins
2 tablespoonsful pea flour
2 tablespoonsful brown rice flour
2 cupsful thick santan
   (page 109)
½ teaspoonful pure vanilla essence
4 tablespoonsful raw cane sugar
⅔ cupful thin santan (page 109)
A few chopped nuts to garnish

1. Wash and dry fruit.

2. Sieve the pea and rice flour together into a mixing bowl. Stir in a little of the thick santan to form a smooth paste.

3. Stir in the remaining thick santan, dried fruit, vanilla essence and sugar.

4. Pour the thin santan into a small saucepan and bring just to the boil. Remove from heat and pour slowly into the flour mixture, stirring all the time, until the porridge is thick and creamy.

5. Serve in individual bowls, either hot or cold, decorated with a few chopped nuts.

SESAME SEED CAKES

Imperial (Metric)	American
1 lb (455g) plain wholemeal flour	4 cupsful plain wholewheat flour
½ teaspoonful baking powder	½ teaspoonful baking soda
2 eggs	2 eggs
4 oz (115g) polyunsaturated margarine	½ cupful polyunsaturated margarine
4 oz (115g) raw cane sugar	⅔ cupful raw cane sugar
4 oz (115g) sesame seeds	⅔ cupful sesame seeds

1. Sift the flour and baking powder onto a pastry board. Make a well in the middle of the flour and break one egg into this; add the margarine, cut into small pieces, and sugar.

2. Gently work the flour into the centre until a dough is formed; knead for 5 minutes.

3. When dough is thoroughly kneaded, roll it into a long cylinder about 1 in. (2.5cm) in diameter. Cut into 1 in. (2.5cm) lengths and roll each of these segments into a ball with the palms of your hands, flattening them to form ½ in. (1.25cm) disks.

4. Separate the other egg. Beat the yolk with a fork and brush the top surface of each disk with this.

5. Spread sesame seeds on a plate and drop each disk (wet side down) into the seeds. Press the dough into the seeds gently, turn the cakes the other way up and lightly brush with the egg white.

6. Place the seeded cakes on a lightly greased baking sheet (plain side down) and bake in a moderate oven 375°F/190°C (Gas Mark 4) for about 15 minutes until the cakes are golden brown.

COCONUT BALLS

Imperial (Metric)	American
½ lb (225g) dried green peas	1¼ cupsful dried green peas
2 tablespoonsful soft raw cane sugar	2 tablespoonsful soft raw cane sugar
4 oz (115g) desiccated coconut	1¼ cupsful desiccated coconut

1. Soak the dried peas in a basin of cold water for 30 minutes, drain, rinse under running cold water and then cook in fast-boiling water until soft.

2. Drain thoroughly, place in a mortar and pound to a smooth paste. Add the sugar and half the desiccated coconut, mix well.

3. Divide the mixture into even-sized portions and roll each into a ball using the palms of your hands. Roll each ball in the remaining coconut to coat and serve cold.

Note: An alternative is to use all the coconut for the ball mixture and then to coat each ball in batter and deep-fry before serving hot, with or without syrup.

SWEET SOUP GLOBES

Imperial (Metric)	American
½ lb (225g) fine maize flour	1½ cupsful fine cornmeal
½ lb (225g) glutinous brown rice powder	1½ cupsful glutinous brown rice powder
½ lb (225g) black bean paste	1 cupful black bean paste
½ lb (225g) raw cane sugar	1⅓ cupsful raw cane sugar
1 large piece fresh ginger	1 large piece fresh ginger
3 pints (1.7 litres) water	7½ cupsful water

1. Slowly add a little water to the maize flour (cornmeal) and knead into a soft dough. Add rice powder and continue to knead until well blended.

2. Break off pieces of the dough and roll each piece in the palms of your hands until it has all been rolled into balls about the size of walnuts.

3. Roll the black bean paste into a long cylinder about ½ in. (1.25cm) in diameter. Cut off sections about ½ in. (1.25cm) in length and roll these in your palms in to small pellets.

4. Take a dough ball, flatten it in the palm of your hand and place a bean pellet neatly in the centre. Roll the dough ball up around the pellet, press the edges firmly together and roll gently in your palms to regain its ball shape. (It is essential that the black bean filling is completely sealed within the dough case.) Repeat the process until all the dough and filling has been used.

5. Crush the brown sugar in a mortar and then boil it in a large saucepan with the piece of ginger in 3 pints (1.7 litres/7½ cupsful) of water. Once the syrup reaches boiling point, turn down the heat to the lowest possible point and drop the dough balls in very carefully.

6. Continue cooking on a very low flame until all the balls float to the surface. Simmer for a further 10 minutes and serve hot by ladling the syrup-coated balls into heated bowls.

VERMICELLI PUDDING

Imperial (Metric)
½ lb (225g) fine wholemeal
   vermicelli
2 tablespoonsful sesame oil
2 pints (1.15 litres) milk
4 tablespoonsful raw cane sugar
2 oz (55g) sultanas
1 oz (30g) pistachio nuts or peanuts
1 tablespoonful sesame seeds, dry
   roasted

American
8 ounces fine wholewheat vermicelli
2 tablespoonsful sesame oil
5 cupsful milk
4 tablespoonsful raw cane sugar
⅓ cupful golden seedless raisins
2 tablespoonsful pistachio nuts or
   peanuts
1 tablespoonful sesame seeds, dry
   roasted

1. Break the vermicelli into small pieces and roast in a pan with half the sesame oil for about 5 minutes until golden brown.

2. Add the milk and bring quickly to the boil. Reduce the heat and simmer for 10 minutes. Add the sugar and continue cooking gently for a further 15 minutes, stirring frequently.

3. Heat the remaining oil in another pan, add the sultanas (golden seedless raisins) and fry for 3-4 minutes. Add the nuts, continue cooking for a further minute and then mix all the ingredients together in a serving bowl, sprinkle with the sesame seeds and serve hot or cold.

ALMOND LAKE

Imperial (Metric)	American
1 pint (570ml) water	2½ cupsful water
Tin of evaporated milk	Can of evaporated milk
1 tablespoonful cornflour	1 tablespoonful cornstarch
1 teaspoonful pure almond extract	1 teaspoonful pure almond extract
A few drops pure vanilla extract	A few drops pure vanilla extract
1 tablespoonful raw cane sugar	1 tablespoonful raw cane sugar

1. Bring water and evaporated milk to the boil in a saucepan. Reduce heat.

2. Mix the cornflour to a smooth paste with a little of the liquid taken from the saucepan, add to the pan and simmer, stirring continuously, until mixture thickens. Add the flavourings, stir in the sugar and continue to simmer, stirring occasionally, until the mixture has the consistency of custard (about 20 minutes).

3. Serve in individual bowls, hot or cold. Garnish with chopped nuts if desired.

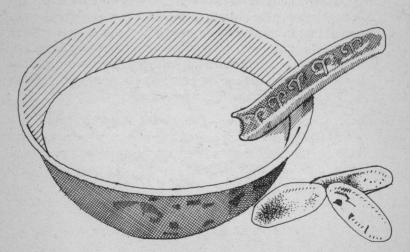

JAVANESE FRUIT SALAD

Imperial (Metric)	**American**
Rojak sauce (page 112)	Rojak sauce (page 112)
2 tablespoonsful vegetable oil	2 tablespoonsful vegetable oil
½ lb (225g) yellow bean curd	8 ounces yellow bean curd
1 small cucumber	1 small cucumber
1 yam	1 yam
Lemon juice	Lemon juice
2 star fruits or 4 rose-apples	2 star fruits or 4 rose-apples
2 mangoes	2 mangoes
Small fresh pineapple (or small tin pineapple cubes in natural juice)	Small fresh pineapple (or small can pineapple cubes in natural juice)
4 oz (115g) fresh bean sprouts	4 ounces fresh bean sprouts

1. Prepare the Rojak sauce and place in the refrigerator to chill.

2. Heat the oil in a pan, fry the bean curd until golden brown on both sides, drain and cut into small cubes.

3. Wash and peel the cucumber, cut into quarters lengthwise, then chop into thick triangles; wash and peel the yam, cut into thick slices, then cut again into triangles and sprinkle these with lemon juice. Wash the star fruits or rose-apples and mangoes, remove skins and seeds, cut into small wedges. If fresh pineapple is used, cut off the skin with a sharp knife, remove the 'eyes', cut into rings, remove the core and cut each ring into small cubes. Wash the bean sprouts, drain, and top and tail.

4. Either arrange the fruits and vegetables in separate heaps on a serving plate and serve the chilled Rojak sauce in a separate bowl or mix all the ingredients together and pour the sauce over them before serving slightly chilled.

AGAR-AGAR DELIGHT

Imperial (Metric)	**American**
4 oz (115g) agar-agar	4 ounces agar-agar
1 pint (570ml) water	2½ cupsful water
Small tin evaporated milk	Small can evaporated milk
6 oz (170g) raw cane sugar, powdered in grinder	1 cupful raw cane sugar, powdered in grinder
Few drops natural food colouring (not cochineal)	Few drops natural food colouring (not cochineal)
Juice of 1 lime or lemon	Juice of 1 lime or lemon
1 egg white, stiffly beaten	1 egg white, stiffly beaten

1. Soak agar-agar in cold water for 20 minutes, drain, then boil in the water until it has all dissolved.

2. Add sugar to the liquid, stir until it dissolves, add milk and continue stirring until the liquid boils.

3. Remove pan from the heat, pour liquid through a fine sieve into a mixing bowl or jug. Add one or two drops of food colouring and strained lime juice; leave to cool.

4. When mixture is cool and just beginning to set, fold in stiffly beaten egg white, pour into wetted, shallow mould and chill in fridge.

5. When set, cut into triangles and serve.

FRIED BANANA CAKES

Imperial (Metric)	American
2 tablespoonsful plain wholemeal flour	2 tablespoonsful plain wholewheat flour
¼ teaspoonful sea salt	¼ teaspoonful sea salt
4 bananas	4 bananas
1 tablespoonful raw cane sugar	1 tablespoonful raw cane sugar
Vegetable oil for deep-frying	Vegetable oil for deep-frying

1. Sieve the flour and salt into a mixing bowl.

2. Peel the bananas and mash them to a pulp with the sugar.

3. Add the sieved flour and salt to the mashed bananas gradually, stirring with a wooden spoon, until the mixture is thick enough to drop easily when shaken from the spoon. (If too thick, add a little cold water; if too thin, add a little more sieved flour.)

4. Heat the oil to haze point and drop the mixture into it gently, a tablespoonful at a time. Continue to fry until golden brown.

5. Remove the banana cakes from the pan, drain on to absorbent paper and serve hot or cold, with or without thin syrup or honey.

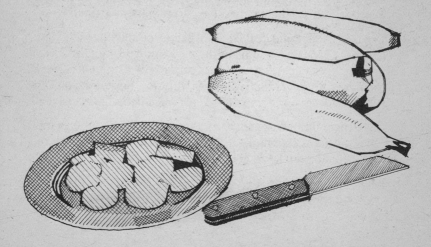

EIGHT TREASURES RICE

Imperial (Metric)	American
1 lb (455g) glutinous brown rice	2 cupsful glutinous brown rice
4 oz (115g) polyunsaturated margarine	½ cupful polyunsaturated margarine
2 oz (55g) raw cane sugar	⅓ cupful raw cane sugar
2 oz (55g) lotus seeds	2 ounces lotus seeds
4 oz (115g) almonds or walnuts, shelled	1 cupful almonds or English walnuts, shelled
4 oz (115g) dragon eyes or raisins	⅔ cupful dragon eyes or raisins
8 Chinese plums or stewing prunes	8 Chinese plums or stewing prunes
2 oz (55g) candied peel	⅓ cupful candied peel
2 oz (55g) crystallized cherries	⅓ cupful crystallized cherries
4 oz (115g) dates	½ cupful dates
1 oz (30g) angelica	2 tablespoonsful angelica

1. Boil glutinous rice until all the water has evaporated. Reduce heat and carefully add the margarine and sugar, blending well with a wooden spoon. Cover pan and leave to simmer until the rice is almost cooked.

2. Meanwhile, blanch the lotus seeds and almonds; wash and pit all the fruits, cut the smaller into halves and the larger into quarters; cut all the candied fruits into narrow strips.

3. Grease a jelly mould heavily with margarine and line with a layer of cooked rice. Press some of the pieces of fruit, nuts and seeds into this layer of rice (try to make a pattern with different colours), then carefully cover this fruit layer with rice. Repeat the process, ending with a layer of rice, until all the ingredients have been used.

4. Place the mould in a steamer and steam for 30-40 minutes until the pudding is set and heated right through. Turn out on to a heated plate and serve hot.

Note: Health food shops stock peel, cherries and angelica prepared with raw cane sugar and without chemical preservatives.

8.

SAUCES AND CHUTNEYS

CHINESE GRAVY

Imperial (Metric)
2 small red onions
3 thin slices fresh ginger
1 tablespoonful cornflour or green
  pea flour
½ pint (285ml) vegetable stock or
  water
2 tablespoonsful soya sauce
1 tablespoonful vegetable oil

American
2 small red onions
3 thin slices fresh ginger
1 tablespoonful cornstarch or green
  pea flour
1⅓ cupsful vegetable stock or water
2 tablespoonsful soy sauce
1 tablespoonful vegetable oil

1. Wash, peel and slice onions and ginger.

2. Blend the thickening to a smooth paste with a little of the stock
   or water.

3. Add rest of liquid and soya sauce.

4. Heat oil and fry onions and ginger slowly without browning.

5. Pour all the liquid on to the fried onions and ginger, bring to
   the boil, stirring all the time, until the gravy is clear and has
   thickened. Serve with noodles, boiled rice or cooked vegetables
   such as cabbage.

PEPPER WATER

Imperial (Metric)	American
1 teaspoonful coriander seeds	1 teaspoonful coriander seeds
1 teaspoonful anise	1 teaspoonful anise
1 teaspoonful cumin powder	1 teaspoonful cumin powder
2 dried red chillies	2 dried red chillies
3 small red onions	3 small red onions
½ tablespoonful vegetable oil	½ tablespoonful vegetable oil
¼ teaspoonful mustard seeds	¼ teaspoonful mustard seeds
1 curry leaf	1 curry leaf
1 tablespoonful tamarind	1 tablespoonful tamarind
¼ pint (140ml) warm water	⅔ cupful warm water

1. Lightly grind the coriander, anise, cumin, chillies and skinned onions separately.

2. Heat oil and fry mustard seeds, ground chillies and curry leaf.

3. Add all other ground ingredients and fry lightly.

4. Mix tamarind with warm water and add to other ingredients in pan.

5. Bring gently to the boil. Serve with curries and rice.

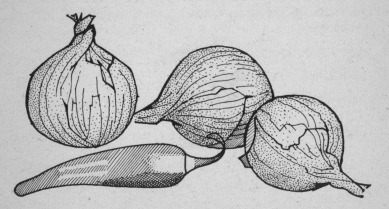

SANTAN (COCONUT MILK)

Imperial (Metric)	American
1 coconut	1 coconut
½ pint (285ml) water	1⅓ cupsful water

1. If necessary, remove husk from coconut. Split nut across the middle and discard the liquid.

2. Use a scraper to remove the flesh from both halves of the coconut on to a clean plate, taking care not to include the dark inner lining of the shell.

3. Divide the scraped coconut into two portions and set one aside. Pour half the cold water over half the coconut and mix well using your hand.

4. Place a fine strainer over small basin and, squeezing firmly, allow the coconut milk to drip into the bowl. Set squeezed coconut aside and repeat straining process with remainder of scraped coconut mixed with the rest of the water in same way.

Note: This first, thick extraction is used for thickening curries, sauces etc. A second, thinner extraction can be obtained by repeating steps 3 and 4 using the already squeezed coconut. This is used for flavouring soups, puddings and sauces etc.

VEGETABLE STOCK

Imperial (Metric)	American
1 lb (455g) any root vegetable	1 pound any root vegetable
1 small onion	1 small onion
1¾ pints (1 litre) water	4½ cupsful water
1 teaspoonful sea salt	1 teaspoonful sea salt
¼ teaspoonful freshly ground black pepper	¼ teaspoonful freshly ground black pepper

1. Clean all vegetables thoroughly and cut into thin slices.

2. Bring water to boil in large pan, add vegetables and seasoning, simmer gently for 30-40 minutes until vegetables are soft but not broken.

3. Strain carefully, allow to cool and use as basis for soups, sauces etc.

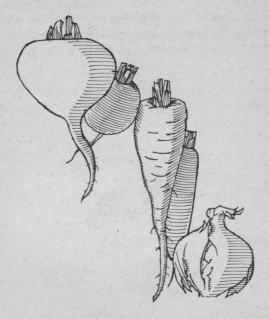

SAMBAL

Imperial (Metric)	American
2 green and 2 red chillies	2 green and 2 red chillies
1 curry leaf	1 curry leaf
2 teaspoonsful mustard seed	2 teaspoonsful mustard seed
2 tablespoonsful desiccated coconut	2 tablespoonsful desiccated coconut
1 tablespoonful wine vinegar	1 tablespoonful wine vinegar
8 small red onions, finely chopped	8 small red onions, finely chopped

1. Wash the chillies, remove their stems but not the seeds, and cut in half lengthwise.

2. Wash the curry leaf and mustard seeds, drain and pat dry.

3. Place the chillies, coconut and mustard seeds in a mortar and grind together until they are very finely ground.

4. Put the ground ingredients in a small bowl, add all the other ingredients and mix together thoroughly. (Extra vinegar can be added to make the sambal of the consistency of thick porridge if desired.)

5. Serve in a small dish with any curry.

ROJAK SAUCE

Imperial (Metric)
3 fresh red chillies, washed and de-seeded
2 oz (55g) peanuts, dry roasted
½ pint (285ml) asam water
2 tablespoonsful raw cane sugar

American
3 fresh red chillies, washed and de-seeded
3½ tablespoonsful peanuts, dry roasted
1⅓ cupsful asam water
2 tablespoonsful raw cane sugar

1. Grind the prepared chillies and peanuts together finely in a mortar.

2. Put the asam in a small saucepan with the sugar and heat gently while stirring until all the sugar has dissolved.

3. Mix all the ingredients together and chill before serving with fruit, salads, noodles or rice.

GADOH-GADOH SAUCE

Imperial (Metric)
1 teaspoonful tamarind
3 tablespoonsful water
2 oz (55g) peanuts, dry roasted
4 fresh red chillies
2 small red onions
1 tablespoonful vegetable oil
⅓ pint (200ml) thick santan
  (page 109)
1 teaspoonful gula malacca
Sea salt to taste

American
1 teaspoonful tamarind
3 tablespoonsful water
3½ tablespoonsful peanuts, dry
  roasted
4 fresh red chillies
2 small red onions
1 tablespoonful vegetable oil
¾ cupful thick santan (page 109)
1 teaspoonful gula malacca
Sea salt to taste

1. Prepare the asam by soaking the tamarind in the cold water, stirring until it has all dissolved. Strain to remove any sediment.

2. Dry roast the peanuts and rub off their skins; wash and seed the chillies; peel and slice the onions finely.

3. Put the chillies and nuts in a mortar and grind coarsely.

4. Heat the oil in a pan, fry the onions until they are soft but not browned, add the ground chillies and nuts and half the santan. Continue to simmer while stirring until the sauce thickens.

5. When the sauce is smooth, add the gula malacca, salt, asam water and the remainder of the santan. Bring back to simmering point, cook for a further 3 minutes, stirring continuously, until the sauce thickens and the gula malacca has dissolved.

Note: This sauce is often served with vegetable dishes as well as with desserts.

SATAY SAUCE

Imperial (Metric)	**American**
2 oz (55g) peanuts	3½ tablespoonsful peanuts
1 tablespoonful coriander seeds	1 tablespoonful coriander seeds
1 teaspoonful anise	1 teaspoonful anise
½ teaspoonful poppy seeds	½ teaspoonful poppy seeds
4 dried red chillies	4 dried red chillies
2 in. (5cm) lemon grass	2 inches lemon grass
2 whole black peppercorns	2 whole black peppercorns
1 in. (2.5cm) fresh ginger	1 inch fresh ginger
2 candle nuts	2 candle nuts
4 small red onions	4 small red onions
1 clove garlic	1 clove garlic
2 tablespoonsful coconut oil	2 tablespoonsful coconut oil
¼ pint (140ml) asam	⅔ cupful asam
1 teaspoonful raw cane sugar	1 teaspoonful raw cane sugar
½ teaspoonful sea salt	½ teaspoonful sea salt
¼ pint (140ml) thick santan (page 109)	⅔ cupful thick santan (page 109)

1. Dry roast the peanuts in a pan, remove their skins and pound lightly in a mortar; set aside.

2. Put the seeds, spices, candle nuts, onions and garlic together in a mortar and grind until fine.

3. Heat the coconut oil to haze point in a pan, fry all the ground ingredients until they separate in the oil. Add the asam, sugar and salt, bring to the boil.

4. Reduce the heat and simmer, uncovered, until the sauce thickens, stirring occasionally.

5. Stir in the coarsely ground peanuts and the santan, simmer while stirring continuously until the sauce thickens further. Pour into a serving dish and leave to cool.

SWEET AND SOUR TOMATO SAUCE

Imperial (Metric)	American
1 tablespoonful cornflour	1 tablespoonful cornstarch
½ pint (285ml) water or vegetable stock	1⅓ cupsful water or vegetable stock
1 tablespoonful cider vinegar	1 tablespoonful cider vinegar
2 tablespoonsful soya sauce	2 tablespoonsful soy sauce
1 tablespoonful raw cane sugar	1 tablespoonful raw cane sugar
2 tablespoonsful tomato ketchup	2 tablespoonsful tomato catsup
1 teaspoonful sea salt	1 teaspoonful sea salt

1. Blend the cornflour to a smooth paste with a little of the water or stock.

2. Add the vinegar, soya sauce and remainder of the water or stock; mix well.

3. Pour into a small saucepan and bring to the boil slowly, stirring all the time with a wooden spoon, until the liquid thickens and becomes clear. Reduce the heat and continue to cook for a further 2-3 minutes to remove the raw flavour of the starch thickening.

4. Add the sugar and tomato ketchup. Continue to cook over a gentle heat until the sugar has dissolved, stirring continuously but gently.

5. Add salt, stir in and remove from heat.

6. This sauce can be served separately with rice, noodles etc., or can be poured over most cooked vegetables.

CHILLI SAUCE

Imperial (Metric)	**American**
6 fresh red chillies	6 fresh red chillies
½ teaspoonful sea salt	½ teaspoonful sea salt
2 tablespoonsful raw cane sugar, powdered in a grinder	2 tablespoonsful raw cane sugar, powdered in a grinder
2 tablespoonsful cider vinegar	2 tablespoonsful cider vinegar
2 tablespoonsful water	2 tablespoonsful water

1. Wash the chillies, remove their stalks and seeds; pound with salt in a mortar until very finely ground.

2. Place the ground chillies in a mixing bowl with the sugar, vinegar and water. Stir well until all the sugar has dissolved. Serve in small Chinese sauce dishes.

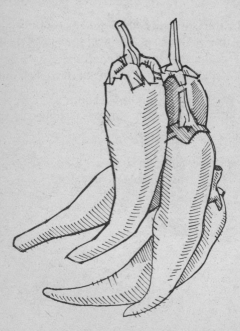

MANGO CHUTNEY

Imperial (Metric)
2 large green mangoes
2 small red onions, finely sliced
2 dried red chillies, de-seeded and
   shredded
1 tablespoonful ghee or vegetable oil
2 tablespoonsful soft raw cane sugar
½ pint (285ml) water
¼ teaspoonful sea salt

American
2 large green mangoes
2 small red onions, finely sliced
2 dried red chillies, de-seeded and
   shredded
1 tablespoonful ghee or vegetable oil
2 tablespoonsful soft raw cane sugar
1⅓ cupsful water
¼ teaspoonful sea salt

1. Wash and peel the mangoes. Cut them in half lengthwise.

2. Melt the ghee in a pan, add the onions and chillies and fry lightly. Add the remaining ingredients, cover and cook over a low heat for 15-20 minutes until the mangoes are soft.

3. Uncover the chutney and continue to simmer, stirring continuously, until it thickens and becomes clear. Serve with curries.

ONION CHUTNEY

Imperial (Metric)   **American**
2 large onions   2 large onions
Lemon juice   Lemon juice
Paprika   Paprika

1. Peel the onions and slice them very thinly. Sprinkle with lemon juice and leave for an hour before serving.

2. Sprinkle with paprika immediately before serving with curries.

Note: Chopped tomatoes or finely shredded cucumber can be added to this chutney if desired.

GLOSSARY

For convenience, this glossary is arranged alphabetically with the name of the ingredient given exactly as it appears in the recipe.

Agar-agar
A gelatinous substance derived from seaweed. Completely tasteless and odourless, it takes longer to dissolve than gelatine but produces a dish that will remain firm.

Anise/Aniseed
Dried, ripe fruit of the anise plant. Highly aromatic, it has a sweetish scent and flavour reminiscent of liquorice. The seeds are similar in shape and flavour to those of the caraway.

Asam (Water)
Sometimes known as pepper-water, asam is obtained by dissolving tamarind in water in a proportion of 2 tablespoonsful of tamarind to every ½ pint (285ml/1⅓ cupsful) of water. It is used as a base for soups, sauces, sambals and curries and has a strangely sweet/sour savour.

(Soya) Bean Curd
One of the staple ingredients of Oriental cooking, bean curd is made from fermented soya beans. Highly nourishing and easily digestible, it can be bought fresh, dried, fried, grilled and boiled.
During the lengthy and complicated curdling process, the bean curd milk separates into different layers and that part which rises to the

top is a different colour and texture from the sediment. The soft, white curd (Japanese: *tofu*) must be squeezed between two plates to remove excess water and left to dry out thoroughly before it can be used in most of the recipes in this book. Therefore try to get the harder, yellow bean curd which is sold in dry cakes or slabs as this can be sliced, shredded or cut into shapes easily before cooking. Both varieties are also available tinned.

Bean Curd 'Paper' Sheets
Paper-thin sheets of fried bean curd which are sold in packs of 10-25 sheets. Very fragile, they need to be soaked for a few minutes before use or they will break (but can be repaired by wetting and overlapping the broken edges).

Black Bean Paste
Thick, syrupy paste made from fermented soya beans and used as a flavouring or as a filling. Usually sold in pots or tins.

Candle Nuts
The fruit of the candleberry tree; these nuts are rich in oil and, if lit, will burn like a candle for up to ½ hour. Any fatty or oily nuts may be substituted in most recipes.

Cardamom
Dried, ripe fruit of the cardamomun. Available whole, from which the seeds can be extracted and used, as seeds or ground. Warming in flavour and smell, they are used in sweet and savoury dishes, particularly curries and pilaus.

Cellophane Noodles
Sometimes called beanthread or transparent noodles, these shiny noodles are made from mung bean flour and really do look as though made of cellophane.

Chinese Dates
Dried, small red fruits with wrinkled, leathery skins which swell when

cooked and taste like dates. Best soaked overnight in cold water before use.

Chinese Plums
Candied plums sold in jars. Sometimes labelled honey-preserved plums, these bright green or red fruits are decorative as well as sweet-tasting.

Cloud Ears
Type of cultivated fungus that looks particularly unappetizing in its dried state. After soaking to obtain its full size, however, it has the appearance of a brown, gelatinous ear or butterfly and has a more pungent flavour than mushrooms.

Coriander
Aromatic fruit of small, hardy annual, this has a delicately refreshing scent and flavour which increase the longer and drier it is kept. The tender, lacy leaves are used as a garnish and in salads.

Cumin
Dried, ripe fruit of a fragrant herb. The seeds look much like caraway but have a harsher, more bitter taste. Used extensively in pilaus and curries, they can be bought whole or ground.

Curry Leaves
These are the leaves of an aromatic bush and have the same taste as garam masala, or a curry powder.

Daikon Radish
Giant white radish with a pungent flavour similar to horseradish which can be used as a substitute if necessary.

Dragon Eyes
A tree fruit similar to lychee but with a softer, smoother skin. Available fresh, tinned (sometimes labelled *loong ngaan* or *longan*) or dried, when they resemble succulent sultanas.

Dried Mushrooms
Chinese dried mushrooms are black-capped mushrooms and expand to full size if soaked in water. Remove the stems for cooking and always wash before soaking. Button mushrooms do not make a suitable substitute.

Fresh Ginger
A tuberous root, fresh ginger is hot and spicy; the older the root the sharper the flavour and the tougher the texture. If recipe calls for fresh ginger and this is not available, use dried which must be soaked before use. Ground ginger has a very different flavour.

Garam Masala
A condiment made from a mixture of ground spices: black peppercorns, dark caraway seeds, cloves, cinnamon, coriander and cardamoms. Used extensively in curries.

Ghee
Clarified butter, used mainly in Indian cooking instead of oil.

Glutinous Rice
A variety of small-grained brown rice which is used to make conjee — rice gruel. Round grain brown rice can be used as a substitute.

Gram Flour
One of a variety of pea or bean flours, this is made from chick-peas (garbanzos) and is available in good healthfood shops.

Gula Malacca
A coarse, thick brown sugar made from various palms. Can be bought in the form of round cakes or already crushed. Used as an ordinary sugar and sometimes soaked and cooked to a thick syrup, it also gives its name to a Malay pudding.

Lemon Grass (*Serai*)
Aromatic grass used extensively in Oriental cooking to impart a fresh,

lemony tang to a dish. It has a bulbous root end, like a young spring onion (scallion), and suitable substitutes are lemon verbena or lemon balm.

Lotus Root
Starchy underwater stem of the water-lily plant. When cut diagonally, the hollow passageways that run lengthways up the stem form circles in each slice. It can be eaten raw, boiled or fried and looks much more attractive once it has been peeled.

Lotus Seeds
Delicate-flavoured seeds which are delicious raw or can be used in cooking. They look like small hazelnuts and have shiny, dark brown husks.

Mangetout Peas
Small green peas which are eaten in their pods. Known variously as mangetout peas, snow peas, French peas, Chinese peas and sugar peas, they must be young and firm or will be tough and stringy when cooked.

Noodles
There are many varieties of noodles: they can be thick, thin, round or flat and may be made from soya beans, buckwheat, wheat flour or rice flour, though the last two mentioned are the most commonly used. They are available fresh or dried and some varieties are transparent (see cellophane noodles). If unobtainable, Italian wholemeal vermicelli can be substituted in many of the recipes.

Poppy Seeds
Tiny, odourless seeds used extensively in Oriental cooking. They have a nutty flavour that becomes more pronounced if the seeds are toasted.

Red Bean Paste
A thick sauce made from soya beans, red rice and salt water; can be bought fresh or tinned.

Rose-Apples
Sometimes known as Malabar plums, the fruits are about the size of a hen's egg; they are rose-scented but taste like apricots.

Saffron
Dried stigmata of the saffron crocus, used as a flavouring and colouring agent for pilaus etc. To release the colour, soak a few strands in water, milk or rose-water before using for culinary purposes. Turmeric also contains a strong yellow dye but, if using this in place of saffron, only use a little as it has a very different flavour.

Sambal
A spicy dish or condiment made from ground red chillies.

Santan
Coconut milk or cream; can be made from fresh or desiccated coconut.

Sesame Seeds
Black or white seeds of an aromatic herb. They have a warm, nutty flavour and, when toasted and ground, taste similar to roasted almonds.

Soya Sauce
This condiment is as important in Oriental cookery as is salt in the West. It has a distinctive smell and salty flavour and can vary in colour according to the soya beans from which it derives.

Star Anise
Eight-pinnacled star-shaped fruit which, when dried, is a rich, burnt sienna colour. Each pod holds a shiny, brown seed which possesses very fragrant, volatile oils that aromatize and flavour the ingredients with which they are cooked.

Star Fruit
Sweet, watery tropical fruit similar to a cucumber but with a star-shaped cross-section.

Tabasco
Condiment made from liquid cayenne pepper which can be used in place of red chillies if these are not available.

Tamarind
Fruit pod of a leguminous tree. It has a sweet-sour flavour and is usually dissolved in water before adding to curries, chutneys, pickles etc. (A mild vinegar can be substituted in some of the recipes.) In appearance, a dark reddish-brown pulp, it is sometimes available fresh but is more frequently sold in jars.

Taucheo
A dry paste, rather like crunchy peanut butter in texture, made from fermented black beans and used as a condiment.

Tiger-Lily Stems
Dried shoots of the tiger-lily plant. Small and brittle until cooked, they look rather like pieces of dried brown noodles.

Transparent Noodles
See Cellophane Noodles.

Turmeric
Fleshy root stalk of a plant belonging to the ginger family. Contains heavy, bright yellow dye and is one of the principle ingredients of curry. Aromatic, with a bitter flavour, it is sold in root form or powdered.

INDEX